Sitting Bull

and the Paradox of Lakota Nationhood

Lakota Chief
American Lakota Sioux Indian Chief

Photographed in 1885 by David F. Barry
Reproduced by permission from The Granger Collection

Sitting Bull

and the Paradox of Lakota Nationhood

by
Gary Clayton Anderson

HarperCollins*CollegePublishers*

Acquisitions Editor: Bruce Borland
Project Coordination and Text Design: York Production Services
Cover Design: Kay Petronio
Manufacturing Manager: Hilda Koparanian
Electronic Page Makeup: York Production Services
Printer and Binder: R.R. Donnelley and Sons Company
Cover Printer: The Lehigh Press, Inc.

Sitting Bull and the Paradox of Lakota Nationhood

HarperCollins® and ☚® are registered trademarks of HarperCollins
Publishers Inc.

Library of Congress Cataloging-in-Publication Data

Anderson, Gary Clayton, 1948–
    Sitting Bull and the paradox of Lakota Nationhood / by Gary
Clayton Anderson.
        p.   cm.—(Library of American biography)
    Includes index.
    ISBN 0-06-501033-7
    1. Sitting Bull, 1834?–1890.   2. Dakota Indians—Biography.   3. Dakota
Indians—Government relations.   4. Dakota Indians—Politics and govern-
ment. I. Title.   II. Series: Library of American biography (New York, N. Y.)
E99.D1S5617   1995
978' .004975' 0092—dc20   95-36261
    [B]   CIP

95 96 97 98 9 8 7 6 5 4 3 2 1

Editor's Preface

In 1885, the long confrontation between two ways of life came to a close. In that year, Sitting Bull signed on to appear in Buffalo Bill's Wild West Show. Along with Annie Oakley and William F. Cody, he appeared in a popular display of vestiges of America's vanished frontier. Wherever it went, the show attracted large audiences eager to see for themselves figures as if in a museum, a museum dedicated to the drama of the winning of the West; a story nearing its end.

Sitting Bull grew up while his people still dominated the vast open plains on the edge of the mountains. Attaining leadership at an early age, he determined to resist encroachments on the territories traditions assigned to his group, and determined also to preserve without change the group's tribal culture with its own communal ethic.

His stubborn resolve brought him and the people he led into a violent confrontation with a force against which he could not successfully contend. The vast hunting grounds across which his hunters roamed nurtured the herds of buffalo necessary for their economy but also stood in the way of adventurers moved by restlessness or greed—fur traders, prospectors for gold, fugitives from justice or family responsibility, missionaries, preachers, and teachers—migrating across the frontier from the Mississippi to the Pacific. The urge to join the Pacific to the Mississippi Valley animated romantic schemes for transcontinental railroads to cut through the lands where the buffalo roamed. Responsibility for maintaining order in the remote regions fell to the United States Army sprinkled in little posts, often out of touch with any chain of command. Frequent clashes and occasional battles such as that at Little Big Horn marked the encounter.

Some tribesmen recognized the inevitable outcome early on. Sitting Bull resisted. Ultimately, he too acknowledged what he could not change. Ironically, he then joined forces with Buffalo Bill who had gained fame as agent for the railroads. This account throws light on the course of the conflict of cultures and its resolution.

—Oscar Handlin

Contents

To W. Eugene Hollon,
mentor and friend

Introduction

We all know that biography shapes history. It gives it a coziness that chronological narrative and statistics lack. But why write a biography of such a man as Sitting Bull? He was merely a nineteenth-century Lakota Indian from a minority culture who never had much of an impact on American society. He never wrote an important book or made a significant scientific discovery. He never left behind a philanthropic organization with his name on it and, in fact, he died in total poverty. Most of the time, he held views often diametrically opposite to mainstream America.

We need to study Sitting Bull because reading about his life forces us to examine the purposes and goals of the dominant culture, the one that most of us call American. It makes us look more critically at the individuals who we see as cultural and political role models. And it causes us to examine in more detail the cultural imperialism explicit in our own American society, for Americans have too often demanded cultural conformity at the expense of the richness of cultural diversity. The tendency to reject such diversity is natural for a nation as young as our own, but it must be recognized that such conformity directly affects the lives of people who we as a nation often conveniently forget in our history books.

In fact, Sitting Bull might be someone who many Americans would like to forget. He rejected virtually everything that the dominant culture deemed of value. He lived in a communal world, in a "precapitalistic" economy, where everyone worked for the benefit of the whole band, or tribe, rather than for themselves. When times of trial appeared, Sitting Bull prayed to several spirits, among them *Wakantanka*. This God never possessed a marble sanctuary, and Sitting Bull spoke to him just as easily on a high hilltop as in a building. When the Americans arrived in his land, Sitting Bull defended his religion and his people. Despite some initial success—in particular the defeat of Lieutenant Colonel George Armstrong

Custer—this defense ultimately cost him his life. At his death in 1890, only a handful of followers viewed Sitting Bull as a hero, a testimony to the strength of the conformists' demands of the American reservation system. Although some American journalists saw something noble in Sitting Bull, they too found him to be an anachronism—a person out of date with the modern world of nineteenth-century America.

But every generation rewrites its history, and our understanding of Sitting Bull has undergone numerous revisions. The first serious journalist to write about this man Sitting Bull was Hamlin Garland—famous for his fictional writing of frontier America in stories such as "Rising Wolf—Ghost Dancer," published in 1899, and "Sitting Bull's Defiance," issued in 1902—who portrayed Sitting Bull as the "noble savage" of a frontier that was about to pass into history. Probably in response to this fiction, William McLaughlin, Sitting Bull's only Indian agent, published *My Friend the Indian* in 1910. Although mostly autobiographical, McLaughlin had much to say about his famous charge, Sitting Bull, whom he depicted as arrogant, foolish, and totally unworthy of leadership. Indeed, McLaughlin's Sitting Bull was a coward who had no right to claim the honor of being even a "noble savage."

Convinced of the obvious injustice of this portrayal, Professor Walter Stanley Campbell (aka Stanley Vestal) of the University of Oklahoma set out to write the first scholarly biography of Sitting Bull in the 1920s. His *Sitting Bull, Champion of the Sioux* was based on several years of oral history collected from various living relatives, including the crucially important nephews of Sitting Bull, White Bull and One Bull. Although more accurate than McLaughlin and surprisingly sympathetic to Sioux religion and society, Campbell's book suffered from the author's literary approach. Sadly, Campbell's *Sitting Bull* can be taken seriously only after perusing the many boxes of documents and oral history accounts that he collected. Even after doing this, however, Campbell's work borders on hero worship, for Campbell came to appreciate too fully the accounts of One Bull and White Bull, both of whom had adopted him by the time the book appeared in 1932.

More recent book chapters and biographies often suffer from the same slanted view. Robert M. Utley's *The Lance and the Shield: The Life and Times of Sitting Bull,* published in 1993, is masterfully researched and written. In much the same sense as Campbell, Utley's Sitting Bull becomes a "champion" of the Sioux. Yet Utley never really answers crucially important questions. What was a "champion" to the Lakota people? Or, more precisely, how does Lakota leadership evolve and to what extent did the individual, Sitting Bull, garner influence in a tribal society rent with factionalism? Second, Sitting Bull's rise to power came during a period of rapid change. American invasion slowly threatened the very existence of the Lakota nation. The relationship of the Sioux people with the American government was molded by conflict! To what degree did Lakota society alter itself politically in order to cope with the American threat, and to what degree did this affect Sitting Bull's status as a political leader?

There can be no doubt that the Lakota people turned to more centralized authority as the threat of American invasion became more prominent. Such a change gave more opportunity to aggressive leaders such as Red Cloud, Crazy Horse, and Sitting Bull. But the need for change evolved slowly, starting in the 1850s after conflict erupted with American troops along the Oregon Trail, and it continued into the early reservation period. At every juncture along the way, Americans became more aggressive in dealing with the Sioux people, either in demanding land through treaties or by virtually invading the Sioux domain, destroying game and stealing resources. More determined and often unified leadership was a natural product of this conflict, and various institutions emerged within Lakota society that provided that leadership.

Yet in an ironic sense, at the very time when more authority and more decisive action became necessary to save the Lakota nation from destruction, the lure of the reservation and its free food attracted more and more Lakota people, producing a growing factionalism that would characterize the reservation years to come and help bring about the final downfall of the Sioux as a sovereign people. This, in essence, was the paradox that Lakota leaders faced—the more Sitting Bull and his followers sought to unify and define Lakota nationhood, the more it seemed so distinctly different from what the Americans had to offer, the more Lakota leadership faced factionalism and decay. For the Lakota people, a tribal society, found it extremely difficult to create a strong central authority even though one was absolutely necessary to fight and survive against the American advance.

Despite such setbacks, Sitting Bull persevered and even at times triumphed. He became the symbol of opposition to a government policy of assimilation, or cultural conformity, that sought as its goal the destruction of a people and their identity. For that reason, we need to remember this man in history, and we need to study him. In the face of overwhelming odds, he continued to believe that his way of life, his religion, his understanding of the world, of life and death itself, were right for him and his people.

But in refusing to accept the dictates of an American government, Sitting Bull came to represent the very antithesis of what Americans came to believe as progress. For though many Americans would challenge the evolutionary theories of Charles Darwin, very few would ever question the notion that America of the late nineteenth and early twentieth century was evolving to an ever-higher plateau. People such as Sitting Bull, indeed, all people of color or foreign culture, had no place in this newly won land. Indeed, to the nineteenth-century American, the Sitting Bulls of America might have been a curiosity, worthy of display, but they were also an embarrassment in a land that worshipped progress. And if we learn anything from the study of history, it is that when human beings become anachronisms in their own land, it is because the dominant people of that land have lost the sense of human goodness that makes life in itself valuable.

Over the years, many friends have helped me come to "my" rendition of Sitting Bull, some knowingly and others unknowingly. Certainly, one of the most helpful was R. David Edmunds from Indiana University, who had published an early volume in the Library of American Biography series. I must especially thank Bruce Borland, my editor at Harper-Collins for patience. Bruce believed in the project from the start. The series editor, Oscar Handlin, did a marvelous job of forcing me to focus on broader issues. This is a better biography than it would have been because of Oscar's help. Donald DeWitt and John Lovett at the Western History Center, University of Oklahoma, helped guide me through the Walter Stanley Campbell Papers. Finally, my friend of many years, Dr. Michael Tate, of the University of Nebraska—Omaha, offered criticism on the final manuscript.

Gary Clayton Anderson

April 10, 1995

University of Oklahoma

Prelude

❖
❖

In the predawn hours of December 15, 1890, a procession of riders dressed in blue descended on the small conclave of buildings that housed Sitting Bull and his people along the Grand River of South Dakota. Sitting Bull was a noted Lakota Sioux chief who had opposed the federal government's reservation assimilation program. The people living with him at Grand River had recently embraced the seemingly violent ghost dance that had reached all the Dakota reserves earlier that fall. Government agents had determined to arrest Sitting Bull and remove him from his people.

As the police arrived and dragged the chief from his house, a crowd assembled that encouraged him to resist. Suddenly, Sitting Bull refused to go. Shots rang out. In a quick and brutal affair, half a dozen of Sitting Bull's followers fell dead along with as many police. The chief, being held firmly by policemen, took several bullets, one in the back of the head. He fell, stone dead, on his face in the dirt. In a twist worthy of a screenplay, the men who killed Sitting Bull were his own relatives, Lakota Indians who wore the badge and uniform of agency police. Many had ridden with the chief during the most riveting moment in his life—on the very day that he had helped destroy Lieutenant Colonel George Amstrong Custer and his troops at the Little Big Horn River.

Sitting Bull's death as well as the subsequent massacre of Lakota Indians at Wounded Knee Creek, an event that came two weeks later, signaled the final doom of the Lakota people as a sovereign nation. In the months that followed, most

Lakota men converted to Catholicism or Protestantism, turned to ranching and farming, and gave up forever thoughts of returning to the world of old—the world of the buffalo hunt, which had been the world of freedom.

Within a few years, the federal government forced "allotment" on the Lakota people, villages being dissolved and the Lakota reservations being divided into individual farms. Reservation thereafter dictated acceptable cultural practices to the Sioux people and forced their children to attend schools where they were allowed to speak only in English. Poverty became the norm for the once proud Lakota people. Since a substantial loss of land base would continue as result of allotment. In those trying years, many Lakotas would remember Sitting Bull. He had dedicated his entire life to the preservation of Lakota nationhood. And when his crusade to save his people had been lost, he chose death rather than live as a reservation Indian.

CHAPTER 1

Lakota Nationhood and the Wasicun *Invasion*

❖
❖

As the American nation invaded the lands west of the Mississippi River, a monumental struggle erupted with the original owners. The Americans saw the land as theirs for the taking since they carried the dual banner of civilization and Christianity. They perceived it as their duty to rid the vast western expanse of "savagery" and "lawlessness" and to institute government. The Indian, despite his ownership of the land, had no place in this new order.

But the American perception of the West was built on false premises. The Indian inhabitants possessed both a sophisticated culture and a workable, though institutionally less visible, government. A sense of nationhood existed, especially among the more mobile plains societies, for unlike their American counterparts, tribal nations on the plains all spoke their own languages, and the uniformity of language bred identity and unity. Common language led to the organization of social and political institutions, such as tribal councils and kinship networks, that brought order to the various nations. Finally, unique religions sprung from the powers that provided for the very existence of the people. Although plains Indian religion remained highly individualistic, each person speaking directly with the Great Spirit, it also focused the individual on doing good for the benefit of the band, the tribe, and ultimately, the nation.

Even though Americans often saw the plains as a virtually unoccupied region, land vested with only occasional native "vagabonds," Sitting Bull and his Lakota or Sioux people knew it as their homeland. Americans would call Sitting Bull's people the Sioux, but in their language they called themselves Lakotas, a word meaning simply "the people."[1] All others were not of the nation and had no right to be on Lakota land or to use its resources. This was especially true for the newly arrived *wasicuns,* as the Lakotas called white people. They were of another land, and they seemed to have little understanding of the sense of order and social and political protocol that existed on the plains.

The sociopolitical structure of the Lakota people evolved from the unique economy that they created. Acquiring horses about 1750, they came to rely almost exclusively on the buffalo hunt, this animal providing key ingredients for diet, material for shelter and clothing, and even stimulation for religious power and ceremony. Although gathered plants would offer yet another food source, the buffalo provided the vast majority of the caloric intake in Lakota diet. Over time, after this movement onto the plains, the Lakotas reached a point where they could not survive as a people without the buffalo, and they defended access to the herds with a vengeance.

Given the immeasurable value of the buffalo, various male societies emerged within Lakota society in the late eighteenth and early nineteenth centuries that saw it as their duty to defend access to the herds. These male societies governed the hunt and helped police the hunting grounds. Soon, political structures evolved within the societies, and occasionally, soci-

---

[1]The term *Sioux* is derivative of a derogatory term employed originally by Cree Indians to identify the Dakota, or eastern Sioux people.

eties competed with each other for honors and prestige. To temper the power of the societies, the people recognized powerful chiefs who inherited their badges of leadership from their fathers. Thus, under the direction of the chiefs' societies, or the collection of elders who sat with the hereditary chief, and the male societies, the Lakota became one of the most successful buffalo-hunting people on the plains, eventually dominating the upper watershed of the Missouri River. These people reached the zenith of their existence about 1830.

It was roughly at this time that a proud father named Sitting Bull had a son who later took the same name. The father and son belonged to the Hunkpapa band of Teton Lakota. This band occupied the vast expanse of territory between the upper Missouri and the Yellowstone Rivers, young Sitting Bull being born on the Grand River in what is today north-central South Dakota.

Roughly numbering three thousand people, the Hunkpapa band followed the buffalo herds from valley to valley, sometimes breaking up into small groups to better facilitate food collecting. But at other times, the collections of families came together to feast and offer praises to their God, *Wakantanka,* for the plenty that surrounded them. Men performed the ultimate penitential sacrifice during the major celebration called the sun dance, a gathering in June that featured feasting, dancing, and courting. These were heady times for the Hunkpapas, for they had adapted a fluid social formation and economy to a difficult, sometimes treacherous, landscape. What's more, they had many close relatives to call on to defend their lands.

The Hunkpapa counted among their close relatives some six other bands who formed the Teton Sioux Tribe. They included the Oglala, Minneconjou, Two Kettles, Brulé, Sans Arc, and Blackfoot Sioux. All seven of these bands were often called the Lakota people for the particular dialect of the Siouan language that they spoke. The bands worked together to extend Lakota tribal influence into the Powder River country to the west after 1830 and the Platte and Republican Rivers to the south. In past centuries, all seven Lakota, or Teton, bands had maintained inconsistent relations with other Sioux tribes to the east, including the Nakota Sioux, or Yankton and Yanktonai tribes, who lived east of the Missouri River, and the Dakota or eastern Sioux, the Sisseton, Wahpeton, Wahpekute, and the Mdewakanton tribes, occupants of what would become Minnesota and Iowa. Although the seven different Sioux tribes spoke unique dialects—Lakota, Nakota, and Dakota—folklore suggests that they once all sat at one council fire, and some intermarriage occurred among them.

To a degree, these seven tribes—Lakota, Yankton, Yanktonai, Sisseton, Wahpeton, Wahpekute, and Mdewakanton—made up a nation of people with similar language, religion, and folklore. Yet in 1830, very little sense of political unity existed among them primarily because individually, in the historic period, they had never faced a serious threat to their existence. Trade constituted the most frequent reason for contact, eastern Sioux groups occasionally traveling west to meet distant relatives and acquire horses from them. On these occasions, Lakotas, Nakotas, and Dakotas sat down, smoked pipes, and inquired of one another's lineage, for all Sioux were related, even if distantly so.

Given the contacts that occurred, information spread rapidly across the plains. Just such a meeting between distant relatives no doubt announced the coming of the first white men, or the *wasicun*. Europeans appeared in the seventeenth century, searching for furs and valuable minerals. A few stayed in Sioux lands, taking Dakota and even Lakota wives, some leaving children who grew to adulthood as Indians.

The Americans who came up the Missouri River in 1803 under the leadership of Meriwether Lewis and William Clark, however, had as their goal the announcement that the plains, or what they called Louisiana, now had a new owner. Since this new owner gave the Sioux presents and promised to look out for the best interests of the Indians, the Lakotas often adopted the Americans and occasionally found a place for them in their kinship system. Though not all the Lakota

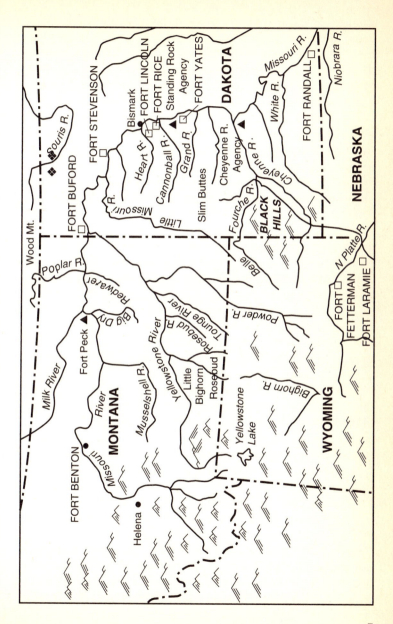

groups viewed the Americans with favor, some band leaders came to call the president of the United States the "Great Father" and visited his spokesman at St. Louis. For the next two decades, these Americans slowly but surely rid the river of other Euroamerican groups, such as the British, who had once traded and lived unmolested among the various tribes.

American penetration of the plains increased in 1822, when William Ashley placed an advertisement in a St. Louis newspaper calling for the enlistment of one hundred "enterprising young men," to follow him up the Missouri. As this fur-trading brigade oared its way into Sioux land, it clashed with the Arikara Indians, a small collection of farmers. The fighting prompted the first American military adventurism on the Missouri, as Colonel Henry Leavenworth marched an army up the river the next year to avenge the attack of the Arikara Indians on Ashley. Leavenworth only partially succeeded in punishing the Arikaras, a conclusion that bothered some traders.

Even though another expedition followed Leavenworth in 1825, reaching the Yellowstone country in eastern Montana, the American army found little to do on the upper stretches of the river and turned it over to the fur traders. As the commerce in skins increased by the end of the decade, additional traders turned to building defensive positions, picking locations along the river that could be served by the newly invented riverboats that increasingly worked the commerce above St. Louis.

Between 1827 and 1832, the American Fur Company consolidated its control over this business, constructing Fort Union at the mouth of the Yellowstone as well as other establishments at various locales downriver. The first Missouri River steamboat, the *Yellowstone,* reached Fort Union in 1832, bringing a new dimension to river travel that the Sioux occasionally found bothersome. Exchanges of goods between the men on board the boats and the Indians frequently went without incident, but at other times, the Sioux came to blame the boatmen for a variety of problems and attacked these steam-breathing giants. The most famous incident of this sort came in

1837 when a steamboat with smallpox on board inadvertently spread the virus among most of the tribes along the river. The agricultural Indians—especially Mandans, Hidatsas, and Arikaras—suffered terrible losses from the disease.

Some Sioux tribes—Yanktons, Mdewakantons, Sissetons, and Wahpetons, especially—had received vaccinations from government doctors, limiting the impact of the epidemic, but others were not as fortunate. The more northwestern Lakota bands suffered mortality rates of 10 to 20 percent. Yet the traders, who had accidentally spread the disease, had no interest in destroying the native populations. Indeed, with the aid of Indian labor, the traders took one hundred thousand pelts a year out of the upper Missouri by 1850. Very likely this had encouraged the overkilling of buffalo, some four hundred thousand dying at the hands of mostly Indian hunters each year.

As the American Fur Company consolidated the fur trade, *wasicuns* invaded Indian lands for other reasons. The traders had reached the Pacific Ocean and returned with magnificent stories of the fertility of a place called Oregon. In this new land of the Willamette Valley, so the story went, the crops grew taller and better than anywhere else. The climate, it was said, could restore broken health and ward off illness. The first pioneers moved wagons along the Oregon Trail in 1841, following the north bank of the Platte River into Wyoming where the trail led through South Pass and beyond the western divide.

In the first few years of trail activity, the Oglala and Brulé Lakota, who frequently hunted along the Platte, looked with amusement and interest on these pioneer families. Unlike the traders, the pioneer families seldom brought whiskey with them, a common cause for disorder. Many times, the Indians ate with the Americans and traded livestock with them. Lakotas served as expert guides, warning the parties of difficulties ahead and telling them where good grass could be found for animals. The Lakota, in particular, gained renown for being able to swim livestock across a swollen river or creek, several such men taking up permanent residence near a growing way station and fur trade post along the trail called Fort Laramie in southeastern Wyoming, where the Platte and Laramie Rivers had to be crossed. Many a present was exchanged as the *wasicuns* learned that the Lakotas could be invaluable in assisting their travels.

Nevertheless, increased travel along the trail did have an impact on game. "The upper tribes," of the Sioux, Indian agent Thomas H. Harvey wrote in 1845, "complain that the buffalo are wantonly killed and scared off." With each passing year, "subsistence" seemed to become more "precarious." The discovery of gold in California in 1848 added to the problems since it put thousands of Americans onto the Platte River Road, most of them being adult males who wasted little time in placating the Indians. As Lakotas and other Indians began demanding compensation for losses, clashes occurred, conflict accelerating throughout the 1850s. Occasionally, trail travelers complied, handing over a cow or some blankets. But just as likely the Americans acted selfishly and refused to listen to the Indians' appeal.

The growing troubles along the Oregon Trail soon became a priority in the War Department in Washington. In 1846, the army established Fort Kearny in south-central Nebraska. Three years later, mounted rifleman began to permanently camp near the old trading post called Fort Laramie. Then in 1851, Washington officials authorized the negotiation of a major treaty in which representatives of the plains tribes joined at Fort Laramie to discuss the Platte River Road. In exchange for $50,000 in annuities each year for fifty years (later reduced by the Senate to ten years), Lakota and other Indian signatories agreed to allow the road to cross Indian lands.

There is little question that the Indians present at Fort Laramie did not understand the implications of the agreement. Other articles, for example, made it possible for the military to add posts and roads on Indian lands when necessary. Clearly, the plains tribes had agreed to listen to proposals only under the hope of limiting the travel west since the trains had frightened the game herds, and the livestock had placed a strain on grazing. Obviously, the agreement that would set major precedents for future relationships between the Indians and the whites had flaws. That the Americans would put much stock in it at all seems ludicrous since only six Lakotas signed the initial treaty, none of them being either Oglalas or Hunkpapas.

The commissioners in charge of the treaty council, David D. Mitchell and Thomas Fitzpatrick, also attempted to determine the boundaries for the various tribes and establish a permanent peace among them. This proved more difficult than getting agreements regarding roads and forts since both men increasingly recognized that the Lakotas and their Cheyenne allies now dominated the high plains. Indeed, since the eighteenth century, the Oglalas, Minneconjous, Sans Arcs, and Hunkpapas had been pushing the Crows out of the Powder River country, gaining valuable hunting grounds. As the winners in this intertribal war, they wanted little to do with a lasting peace. But the negotiators presented this article in a conciliatory manner, and the handful of Indians present, eyeing the presents that would come with "touching the pen" to the document, all agreed. In reality, all that can be said of the treaty is that thereafter the army felt that it had a right to enter Indian lands at will, building forts and roads wherever necessary.

Although the government presence occasionally brought to the plains men of honor and decency, just as likely, many American officials and army officers lacked a sense of morality. The extreme conviction of winning the West for "civilization" often ran heavy in the blood of Americans, military or otherwise, and most Americans possessed a disregard for the humanity of the Indian, and by extension, Indian nationhood. When men with extreme racist views came into positions of power, trouble with the people of the rising Oglala leader Red Cloud and his northern relative, the now young man, Sitting Bull, became inevitable. The first serious clash of this sort occurred at the annuity distribution at Fort Laramie on August 18, 1854.

Camped near the fort late that summer were a group of Mormon immigrants, resting while on their way to Utah. A scrawny cow from their camp wandered off and reached a

Lakota village not far away. A Minneconjou who was visiting with the Brulés promptly butchered the animal and offered a feast. When hearing of the incident, the fort commander sent a young lieutenant named John L. Grattan to seize the poacher and bring him to justice. Unfortunately, the Minneconjou Lakota was a guest of the Brulé chief Conquering Bear, and the chief respectfully refused to surrender him. Grattan, with twenty-eight soldiers, had no intention of being rebuffed by an Indian. He provoked a fight, killing the Brulé chief. As the camp erupted in gunfire, the unsuspecting Sioux quickly garnered reinforcements and dispatched Grattan and nearly two dozen of his men.

While the Mormon cow incident should never have happened, what followed proved even more provocative. In American military circles, the Grattan incident was viewed as a "massacre," warranting revenge. The army selected one of its most seasoned commanders to carry out this punishment—Colonel William S. Harney. Harney had few redeeming characteristics, being a huge man with hard convictions. In addition, he thoroughly disliked Indians, the Lakotas later giving him the nickname "Mad Bear." In the fall of 1855, Harney determined to strike the nearest Sioux village revenging the death of Grattan and his men. Soon news reached him of a large hunting camp located in the Platte River valley, well west of his station, Fort Leavenworth. In late summer, he led his heavily armed troops out of the fort, intending to surprise the village and kill Indians.

After a considerable march, a camp of 250 Brulé Sioux lay before Harney near a small tributary of the North Platte called Ash Hollow. The Brulé leader Little Thunder, successor to Conquering Bear, had little reason to suspect what Harney intended, for he was camped on his own land, peacefully hunting. As was customary, Little Thunder came forward with a flag of truce to meet Harney. But when promptly served with terms of unconditional surrender, Little Thunder vacillated. Harney then pitched into the camp, the general later reporting that his men killed eighty-six Indians (other reports put the number at well over one hundred). Seventy women and children were spared, but one infantryman reported that "we, of necessity, killed a great many women and children." The first premeditated "massacre" in what would become the great Sioux war was clearly perpetrated by American soldiers on Lakota Indians.

Harney then marched overland to Fort Laramie and eastward back to the Missouri, seemingly surveying the Cheyenne River valley but in effect invading the heartland of Lakota hunting lands. Harney's trip came to be characteristic of the lack of regard that the American military and government held for Indian land rights. Near Fort Pierre on the Missouri, Harney sent out word that winter that he wished to see all the Lakota leaders in council. In early March, he assembled the various northern Lakota tribes, some delegates being present from the Minneconjous and Hunkpapas, and forced them to sign yet another treaty. It proclaimed that the Indians would surrender stolen property and hand over any tribesman guilty of killing whites. Moreover, in what was clearly a ridiculous notion, Harney demanded that each Lakota band select a leader to represent them. This man would answer to the Americans for any crime and keep his people in line.

Many Lakota leaders had little understanding of what Harney wanted, and Hunkpapa spokesman, Bear's Rib, tried unsuccessfully to make the general aware that such a request was impossible. It violated the sanctity of the Lakota political system, which made decisions through band or tribal councils. Yet Harney got his way and even convinced Bear's Rib to accept a commission as head chief of the Hunkpapas, a role that he misunderstood and was uncomfortable in assuming. As the ceremony depicting his inauguration occurred, nine other leaders were brought forward to assist the Hunkpapa spokesman in keeping order. Among them were Four Horns, Sitting Bull's uncle. The Minneconjou then followed, selecting Sitting Bull's brother-in-law, Make's Room, father to the young boys White Bull and One Bull. Since Sitting Bull, Four Horns, White Bull, and Make's Room were often inseparable, the emerging Hunkpapa leader very likely witnessed this solemn ceremony, it constituting the first time that the Hunkpapas had negotiated as a band with the United States.

Harney concluded his visit at Fort Pierre by promising presents and agricultural implements. Unfortunately, he had no authority to do so, and the Senate ultimately ignored his treaty. Very likely, Harney's selection of "chiefs" among the Lakota had a similar effect among the Indians. They undoubtedly spent many hours debating the merits and meaning of all that Mad Bear had to say. While proceeding downriver later that summer, Harney built Fort Randall, in the lands of the Yankton Sioux, near where the river enters into modern-day Nebraska. Other separate treaties were signed with the Yanktons to facilitate the occupation of their lands. Within a year, the government had established the first Indian agencies for the Yanktons, the Missouri River becoming a conduit for negotiation and for the distribution of goods.

As the military presence increased along the Missouri River, more and more *wasicuns* followed the soldiers. White settlements sprung up at Sioux City, Iowa, and pioneers opened farms on both sides of the Big Sioux River, extending their occupation northward into present-day South Dakota. Further expansion occurred in Minnesota, where the federal government negotiated two treaties in 1851 that opened for settlement virtually the entire southern half of the state, lands previously owned by the eastern Sioux. Farms soon appeared all along the Minnesota River as far west as New Ulm, and some settlers even pushed out onto the southeastern prairie lands of Minnesota, which became a new state in 1858.

By the eve of the American Civil War, all this activity had created considerable resentment among some Sioux groups. Feuding broke out among the Yanktons, some tribal members resenting the sale of their lands. Yanktonais, living just to the north, also criticized their close relatives for selling lands. Even the eastern Sioux—Mdewakantons, Sissetons, Wahpetons, and Wahpekutes—came to regret the treaties that their leaders had reluctantly signed. They had been assigned a small reservation along the upper Minnesota River after selling their lands, but they soon found it inadequate, and much of the food and clothing promised by the government in the treaties had been given to Indians who settled on individual farms, angering those Indians who maintained native ways and hunted. There is little doubt that the most discontented Indians among the middle and eastern Sioux made their way to the council fires of the Lakotas, telling them of their predicaments and advising them to resist the advancing Americans.

The first reactions to these problems came along the Missouri River, where by 1860, Hunkpapas, Brulés, Minneconjous, and Oglalas began attacking small parties and steamboats. A war party of Hunkpapas even tried to overrun Fort Union on one occasion, making it known to many of the traders that they wanted all *wasicuns* to leave their lands. Other Lakotas attempted to break up the annuity distribution at the Yankton Agency the next year. But the instigators of most of these troubles, the white settlers and overland travelers, ignored these signs of discontent. More came every year, especially after 1860. Two motivating factors sent them west—gold had recently been discovered in Montana, and the Civil War kept producing ever-expanding casualty lists, making potential struggles with Indians pale by comparison to military service.

Unfortunately for the Sioux, the gold fields existed well north of the Oregon Trail. By spring 1862, wagon trains left Minnesota, opening a new road through the Dakotas to the mining districts via the Missouri River. Army officers had explored much of this route, and local newspapers, in the spirit of western boomerism, pronounced the road both feasible and safe. Yet another road into the mining lands was begun at Fort Laramie. Named for John Bozeman, the freighter who pioneered it, the trail meandered north through the low-lying Powder River mountains and finally turned west intersecting with the upper Yellowstone River before proceeding into the Rocky Mountains. Westerners saw economic opportunities tied to these roads and raved of their development. And the Indians, they concluded, would simply have to give way to this American advancement or be exterminated.

But many Indians had different ideas. As the dawn broke at the Lower Sioux Indian agency along the upper Minnesota River on August 18, 1862, the shadows revealed lines of armed warriors descending on the buildings. These eastern Sioux had suffered through the long winter, often going without food, even though the agency warehouses possessed ample supplies. But the food available seemed to be given only to "farmer" Indians and loafers who remained about the buildings. Now in late summer, on a morning when severe thunder and rain seemed eminent, still the government had failed to deliver annuities to the majority of Mdewakantons, Wahpekutes, Wahpetons, and Sissetons, and these warriors came to take what they needed to feed their families.

With clouds swirling above, nearly three hundred eastern Dakotas, led mostly by Little Crow, sacked and burned the agency and killed nearly every American connected to it. War parties then proceeded into the countryside, killing *wasicuns* and burning farms everywhere within a one-hundred-mile radius. Thousands of settlers fled east, but about four hundred died in the ensuing fighting. Within weeks, the federal government recognized that a state of war existed with most of the Sioux tribes. As the armies of blue and gray engaged each others ferociously in the east, the War Department met the new crisis in the west by organizing the Military Department of the northwest.

The new department fell under the command of General John Pope, a Union veteran who had been discredited in the Civil War campaigns. The department's first task was to drive the eastern Sioux out of Minnesota. Henry Hastings Sibley, an ex-fur trader who through graft had made a small fortune during the 1851 treaty negotiation, took command of roughly fourteen hundred men in Minnesota. Moving slowly up the Minnesota River by late September, he drove Little Crow and his people out of Minnesota. Capturing many of the farmer Indians, mixed bloods, and a handful of the more militant groups, Sibley organized a military commission, tried the entire group, and condemned 303 Indians to death. The day after Christmas, 1862, thirty-eight of these men, many of them innocent of any wrongdoing, were hung in masse in the square at Mankato, Minnesota. As the gallows platform dropped, a massive "hurrah" went up from the three to four thousand white spectators. This constituted the largest mass execution in American history and briefly answered the cries for revenge that emanated from the local citizenry.

The next year, Sibley and General Alfred Sully received orders from Pope to punish the eastern Sioux as well as those along the Missouri who had attempted to stop navigation along the river and block the route to Montana. While the generals planned expeditions, many of the eastern Sioux fled west, joining ranks with the Yanktonais and even the Lakotas. Some six hundred eastern Sioux had camped for the winter a mere hundred miles above the old fur trading post at Fort Pierre. Others selected Devil's Lake as a place of rendezvous, and a few even fled into Canada where Little Crow represented them in meetings with the British.

During the spring of 1863, Sibley took the field against these bands. Slowed by 225 mule-drawn wagons, his force of several thousand men crept up the Minnesota River and by late summer had reached the tributaries that fed water westward into the Missouri. A large camp of Hunkpapas, Minneconjous, Yanktonais, and various eastern Sioux bands watched his movements and finally engaged him near Long Lake. Sibley claimed to have killed 150 Indians, a gross exaggeration. The colonel, recently promoted to brigadier general, felt satisfied with his "victory" and retired to the east.

Meanwhile, Sully's progress had been even slower, due to the low level of the Missouri and his inability to obtain supplies. When he finally reached the lands above old Fort Pierre in August, he had almost given up on finding any Indians. What a surprise, then, when a scout rushed in to report a large camp of mostly Yanktonais and Hunkpapas located only a dozen miles away. He sent his cavalry in pursuit, capturing and burning a large village complete with its winter supply of buffalo meat. Sully reportedly killed another 150 Sioux men—the number likely was contrived to match his counterpart, Sibley—and took considerable numbers of women and children captive. Sibley and Sully had punished the Sioux, burning meat supplies and tepees and killing some Indians. But they, along with Little Crow and his people, had also inaugurated the plains wars. There was simply no negotiation possible after the invasion of Indian lands by American armies and the burning of Indian villages. To make matters worse, Sully decided to militarily occupy the old fur trading post, Fort Pierre, in the heart of Hunkpapa lands.

Over the winter of 1863–1864, Sully made even more provocative plans. In order to guard the road into Montana, he campaigned well up the Missouri River, invading the very heartland of the Hunkpapas. By July 1864, his two-thousand-man army had reached the badlands of western Dakota. At the foot of Killdeer Mountain, Sully's troops engaged a large Lakota encampment of several thousand people. In the three-day battle, Sitting Bull and many of his closest relatives heroically fought to defend their land against Sully's invasion, using mostly bows and arrows. But the American troops brought cannons that they used effectively to clear the hills in front of their advance. The Indian defense soon gave way, and eventually the Hunkpapas and their allies fled, many being wounded.

Finally reaching the Missouri River, Sully then inaugurated the second part of his plan. He began the construction of a chain of forts, starting at the mouth of the Yellowstone River, hoping to use these garrisons to drive the Indians away from the road. He first built Fort Berthold, near the mouth of the Yellowstone River. Sully then selected a spot for Fort Rice, located well to the east just above the mouth of the Cannonball River. Along with Fort Pierre, later moved and renamed in Sully's honor, the garrisons represented a giant leap into Sioux land.

Sitting Bull's people and many allied Minneconjous, Sans Arcs, Yanktonais, Sissetons, and Mdewakantons were outraged and openly plotted against the forts. By the fall of 1864, not a traveler or a herd of animals was safe anywhere near either Forts Berthold or Rice. Bands of Indians numbering several hundred men frequently swooped down on the establishments, killing isolated soldiers and stealing stock. When the soldiers were too strong for them, the Indians attacked steamboats or wagon trains. Many Lakotas, especially the Hunkpapas, seemed determined to force Sully to evacuate the upper Missouri River Valley.

Although most Hunkpapas, Minneconjous, and Sans Arcs remained committed to expelling the Americans, other Sioux groups grew weary of the war. The Sissetons, Wahpetons, some Mdewakatons, and even many Yanktonais discovered that they were ill prepared to face cannons and heavily armed soldiers with the few muzzle-loading trade guns that they possessed. The more eastern Sioux groups also found it difficult to dodge the large military forces each summer at a time when it was necessary to secure buffalo meat and prepare for the difficult winter. Throughout 1864–1865, then, Sioux factions from a multitude of different bands and tribes turned increasingly to visiting the newly established agencies along the Missouri River, near the mouth of the Cheyenne River and to the south at Crow Creek, where government agents received them and distributed some food and clothing, annuities promised under previous treaties.

Despite these modest successes, the military situation in the west continued to deteriorate for the government. Though Sully had successfully established a chain of forts along the Missouri, the efforts of the government to duplicate that feat farther west along the Bozeman Trail proved increasingly costly and dangerous. Major General Patrick E. Connor had been assigned the task of protecting the trail from Indians. Connor worked under extremely difficult conditions, not the least of which was the fact that the government had utterly failed to negotiate with any of the Lakota tribes for the right to use the road into Montana. When he arrived at Fort Laramie in the spring of 1865, he found the Indians to be in a state of war. But with troops coming in fresh from the Union victory in the east, Connor hoped to quickly clear the entire Powder River area of Indians. Campaigning throughout the summer and into the next winter, he soon found that such a goal was impossible with the men and supplies that he had been allotted.

The Oglala leader Red Cloud had become Connor's primary nemesis. Red Cloud, principally a renowned warrior who had aspirations of one day being recognized as a hereditary chief, had opened talks with the southern Cheyenne in 1865. Here he heard firsthand their account of the infamous Sand Creek massacre. Several hundred Cheyennes and Arapahos had settled at Sand Creek in southeastern Colorado after the army had assured them of the region's safety. Unfortunately, a vengeful colonel in the Colorado militia named John Chivington had no intention of honoring this sanctuary. He attacked the village and killed several hundred people. Given the actions of Chivington, Red Cloud had found it easy to convince many Brulés, Sans Arcs, and even Hunkpapas to join in the fighting. General Connor, plagued by poor weather and supply difficulties, failed utterly by the spring of 1866 to clear the Powder River watershed of the Sioux. His growing problems prompted sentiments for peace negotiation.

The task of convincing the Sioux to allow wagons on the Bozeman Trail fell to Colonel Henry Maynadier who took command at Fort Laramie in the spring of 1866. He convinced several of the annuity Indians living near the post to approach the various Oglala and Brulé bands and ask them to come to the fort and negotiate. The Brulé leader Spotted Tail appeared first, followed shortly thereafter by Red Cloud. Maynadier seemed sure that a deal could be struck since the winter had also been hard on the Lakota, and buffalo seemed scarce that spring. But at a council held in June, Red Cloud, Man-Afraid-of-His-Horses, and several other Oglalas suddenly bolted from the scene since they heard of the arrival of a large military force from the south. Obviously, they had fears of another

Sand Creek. Despite the setback, Maynadier and other commissioners went ahead with a treaty that guaranteed American access to the road in exchange for annuities. None of the
leading Sioux chiefs signed the accords.

Fearing trouble from Red Cloud and others, the army ordered Colonel Henry B. Carrington to accomplish the task earlier assigned to General Connor. Carrington built several new
military posts along the trail, the most crucial being Fort Philip
Kearny, between the forks of the Piney, and Fort C. F. Smith,
nearly a hundred miles to the north in the Big Horn River valley. The army assigned infantry troops to complete this assign-
ment, armed with muzzle-loading muskets. Many soldiers
had as few as eight rounds of ammunition and seldom took
target practice. As the stockades took shape, Lakota Indians increasingly struck at the livestock necessary to freight supplies
into the isolated garrisons. Carrington meanwhile busied himself with the details of construction and gave little attention to
the warnings of his head scout, mountain man Jim Bridger,
who reported that the Sioux were ready for war.

By winter, Lakota parties of several hundred men kept
watch over the new posts, attacking wagon trains along the
road and harassing wood details and herders. During one of
these attacks near Fort Phil Kearny, Carrington ordered Captain William J. Fetterman and two platoons to ride to the relief
of the wood cutters. But Fetterman, a bragger who once said
that with just a hundred men he could raid through the entire
Sioux nation, exceeded his orders and followed the retreating
decoys several miles beyond the fort. As the racing cavalry
troop passed out of sight of Colonel Carrington, it fell into an
ambush in which all eighty men were killed. The Oglala in
charge of the decoy group was none other than Crazy Horse.
Other Hunkpapas and Minneconjous joined in the triumph.

The Fetterman "massacre," as the newspapers called it,
shocked the army and the nation. Fetterman's troops had been
poorly armed and led. At first, the outrage led to cries for revenge. General William Tecumseh Sherman at the War Department, an officer known for drastic measures, declared that "at

least ten Indians" should be killed for every soldier lost. He cared little whether the victims had been involved in the Fetterman fight or not. Any Indians would do. But Congress generally disagreed, as did officials at the Bureau of Indian Affairs. Critics argued that perhaps the soundest policy would be to simply abandon the Powder River country to the Indians. Treaties could then be negotiated in which reservations could be assigned to each tribe—even those unwilling at least initially to settle on one—and the Indians ultimately convinced to begin farming.

Following the arguments of these men, Congress created a peace commission in July 1867. Headed initially by Commissioner of Indian Affairs, N. G. Taylor, the delegation included leading advocates of a reservation policy, as well as several military generals. When they reached the west, the commissioners discovered that conditions had deteriorated. Lakota war parties virtually controlled the Powder River country, sending smaller groups as far west as the Gallatin River Valley in the Rocky Mountains. Wagon trains had little chance of safely reaching Montana via the Bozeman Trail, and few even tried. When approached with offers of peace, Red Cloud and other Lakota leaders simply replied that they would negotiate only after the three forts in the Powder River country had been abandoned. Realizing that the road had become somewhat obsolete after the completion of the Union Pacific Railroad—trains were then reaching the Rocky Mountains—the commission finally relented and accepted these terms.

Over the next year, the peace commission made slow progress in convincing the Lakota to sign a treaty. The army caused the delay, abandoning the forts very slowly over the spring and summer of 1868. But as this process got underway, group after group of Indians came into Fort Laramie and signed a new treaty. The Brulés under Spotted Tail came first. Of course, they had little claim to land in the west. Finally by November, after most other Oglala leaders had signed the treaty, Red Cloud appeared and made his mark. Several prominent Hunkpapas, including Running Antelope and

Bear's Rib, ultimately signed the agreement. But the signatures of the major Hunkpapa leaders, including Sitting Bull and Four Horns, were conspicuously absent.

Despite the extended role that Red Cloud had played in setting the terms and negotiating this treaty, even he seemed totally unaware of what had been agreed on. Although the opening paragraphs of the agreement talked of peace, the fine print that followed indicated that the Indians had little understanding of the treaty. Most of the treaty dealt with the establishment of reservations for the Indians. Fort Randall on the Missouri River had been selected as the place of distribution for annuities. Obviously, the Oglalas and the Hunkpapas had little intention of traveling that far to collect goods since they were hunters who roamed in the Powder and Big Horn valleys and seldom went that far east.

The most grievous manipulation by the commissioners, however, came in the creation of a "Great Sioux" reservation. The reserve's eastern boundary was established along the west bank of the Missouri River, extending from the northern boundary of Nebraska to the forty-sixth parallel north, a point on the Missouri just below present-day Bismarck, North Dakota. Though this northern boundary cut the Hunkpapas off from some of their best hunting grounds, it did put the northern road into Montana well outside the reservation, and it opened up land for the new Northern Pacific Railroad.

The real travesty in the negotiation came with the creation of the western boundary. The commissioners penciled it in at 104th degree of longitude, or the present western boundary of both North and South Dakota. In other words, in the West the new reservation excluded both the Big Horn and Powder River valleys, the very regions that the Lakota had fought over and demanded that the army evacuate. Few if any Oglala and Hunkpapa leaders had any intention of giving up either the lands north of the reservation west of Bismarck or the valuable hunting grounds along the Powder and Big Horn Rivers. They would not have signed the treaty had they been aware of this line. The commissioners naturally recognized this and simply added article eleven to the document, which gave the Sioux the right to hunt on lands outside the reserve "so long as buffalo may range thereon in such numbers as to justify the chase." The Lakota never understood the temporary nature of this article.

Despite the obvious outrage, the treaty brought a temporary peace to the west. It represented the culmination of what was quickly becoming known as the government's "peace policy," a program advocated by eastern philanthropists in the aftermath of the Civil War. Although the army generally opposed this policy, wishing to pursue "hostiles" anywhere on the Great Plains, Congress concluded that presents and annuities were cheaper than sustained military operations. This new policy contrasted markedly with the earlier actions of Pope, Connor, Carrington, Sully, and Sibley, prompting most of these men to retire or move on to new stations.

The arguments for peace even seemed appealing to territorial officials in the Dakotas. The territorial governor, Newton Edmunds, lobbied Congress in 1865 for the right to negotiate with the various Sioux groups in the eastern portion of the territory. Edmunds believed that more development and profit could come from supplying annuities to the various reservations than in selling food and goods to the military posts necessary to fight the Indians. As anyone could clearly see, there were far more Indians than soldiers along the Missouri River.

While the government moved slowly toward consummating the Treaty of 1868, various small parties of Dakota Indians, well to the east of the Missouri River, returned to the lands that they had once occupied. They understandably demonstrated considerable reticence in dealing with army officials, showing little trust of General Sibley or his adjutants. But they did open negotiations with the various Dakota mixed bloods who occupied scout camps in the James and Big Sioux River valleys.

The most forward of these camps was under the command of Gabriel Renville, who with several dozen Dakota relatives, had selected a spot along Rice Creek, near present-day Wahpeton, North Dakota. Here, Renville spoke frequently with various Sisseton and Wahpeton Sioux leaders and coaxed them ever closer to the negotiation table. In August 1864, General Pope ordered the construction of Fort Wadsworth just west of Big Stone Lake, and within four years, the post had attracted a nucleus of these people. Other Yanktonais negotiated at Fort Pierre and found that the government would feed them if they would live in peace near the Missouri River. As the fighting slowed in the west, and Red Cloud negotiated, Indians living east of the Missouri River signed treaties in which they received reservations and settled into a life of farming and ranching.

Though such a lifestyle did not appeal to most Lakota Indians, the distribution of presents and food made many more friends for the government than did the expeditions of Sully and Sibley. Red Cloud even agreed to travel to Washington, D.C. and visit the president after signing the 1868 treaty. In awkward meetings held at the Interior Department, he soon discovered that the government really wanted him to move his people eastward to the Missouri. He in turn demanded that the army stay out of the Powder River country. In the end, both sides agreed that the interpreters at the treaty had failed to clarify just exactly what the treaty meant. The Secretary of Interior decided to leave Red Cloud's people alone, at least for the moment. The Secretary, in a gesture consistent with the peace policy, even suggested that the Indians select a spot somewhere in the upper Platte country for their new agency, the location being much preferred over Fort Randall and the Missouri River.

In turn, Red Cloud went out to visit groups now increasingly identified as the northern tribes and tell them of his trip to Washington. He spoke throughout the late summer and fall of 1870 with various Oglala bands, as well as with Hunkpapas and Minneconjous. He spoke of peace and encouraged some of these people to move farther south and east. But the Hunkpapa especially wanted nothing to do with this advice even though they could see that the buffalo, long the mainstay of their hunting lifestyle, were becoming more difficult to find in numbers. Two years later, Red Cloud again sent a message to the northern tribes, addressing his words especially to Sitting Bull, No Neck, Four Horns, Fire Horse, and Black Moon, the primary Hunkpapa leaders. "Friends," he wrote, "I carried on the war against the Whites with you until I went to see my Great Father. . . . I asked for many things for my people and he gave me those things." Finally, Red Cloud swore: "I shall not go to war any more with the *wasicuns.*"

But try as he may, Red Cloud could not convince the northern Indians to settle at a reservation. The majority of the Hunkpapas, Minneconjous, and even many Oglalas spent their time hunting in the Yellowstone, Powder, and Big Horn River valleys, sometimes wandering as far south as the Cheyenne valley and the Black Hills. Occasionally, a few men would venture into the new agencies taking shape for Red Cloud, on the White River just above the Nebraska line, or for the Brulé leader Spotted Tail, near Fort Randall. But they came mostly to visit.

The curiosity of the northern tribes about the agencies was clearly matched by a strong suspicion of government officials in general. This seemed all the more the case after the government had completed a new agency for them at Sanding Rock, well above old Fort Pierre. The northern tribes had nothing to do with the new post and especially despised the few Hunkpapas, Minneconjous, Sans Arcs, and Yanktonais who stayed there much of the year. The northern Indians wished only to pursue war against their enemies, the Crows and Assiniboins, and to be left alone to hunt. They continued to harass an occasional army patrol and even took some horses from the herds near Forts Rice and Berthold, but they too seemed to be waiting for the next event, unaware of what the government had plans for and, to some extent, confused over the growing pacifism of the once strong war leader, Red Cloud.

At this crucial juncture, Agent J. W. Daniels, then in charge at Red Cloud Agency, elected to approach Sitting Bull and his fellow chiefs and convince them to come in. Daniels had considerable experience with Indians, having been employed in various capacities in Minnesota and eastern Dakota with the Dakota agencies. Daniels traveled north to Fort Peck, Montana, in the fall of 1872, hoping to meet the various recalcitrant Indians and convince them of the generosity and compassion of the government. Unfortunately, he found the Hunkpapa unwilling to meet with him, and the best he could do was to send them messages. In the exchange of information that followed, Sitting Bull made it quite clear that he had no interest in bothering the Americans if they left him alone. And reservation life, at least for him, was out of the question.

As tensions built within the two widely dispersed factions of annuity and nonannuity Indians, frontier boomerism entered a new stage of aggressiveness that threatened to reopen the hostilities that the 1868 Fort Laramie treaty had supposedly ended. There had been rumors for decades of rich gold deposits in the region that the Sioux called the *Paha Sapa,* or the Black Hills. This land, mysterious and religiously important to the Lakota, remained completely within the boundaries of the Great Sioux Reservation. But such restraints had seldom dampened the American frontier spirit and even before the 1868 treaty, handfuls of miners had organized themselves in the frontier communities of Yankton and Vermillion intent on broaching the Black Hills. Although the army issued orders prohibiting the penetration of the region, everyone seemed to sense that it would be difficult to prevent the parties from leaving.

In an effort to prove the rumors false, the army finally concluded to send an expedition into the region and survey the Black Hills. The task fell to Lieutenant Colonel George Armstrong Custer. Already famous for his cavalry exploits during the Civil War, Custer organized his party of several hundred men at the newly constructed Fort Abraham Lincoln, located near Bismarck. They left for the hills on July 2, 1874, the party containing a mile-long baggage train, cavalry and infantry troops, reporters, and at least one mining expert. The Custer party found little real evidence of precious metals, but various men did discover some surface gold, and the newspapers promptly elevated this find to a major strike. Custer seemed uninterested in dissuading the stories and had done more to provoke trouble than stop American entry into the hills.

On the return of Custer, Red Cloud demanded to go to Washington. Although he had opposed the Custer trip, his main reason for speaking with government officials was to complain of the quality of the annuities that had been handed out at the reservation. Yet as soon as Red Cloud, Spotted Tail, and other Oglala and Brulé chiefs met the president in the spring of 1875, the issue of the Black Hills came up. Later the Secretary of Interior even asked the Lakota leaders if it would not be better for them to agree to sell all of their land and move to Indian territory in Oklahoma. Once officials in the Interior Department realized that this idea seemed preposterous to the Sioux, they tried to convince the Indians to sell the Black Hills, arguing in effect that whites would eventually invade it anyway and that the Indians might as well get a good price. Needless to say, Red Cloud and Spotted Tail both went home disappointed with their councils.

On their return from Washington, the Sioux leaders found that more and more whites were pouring into the Black Hills. The army sent in two more military expeditions over the summer, but the soldiers failed to resolve the debate over the quantity of gold found there, and the civilians already in the hills refused to leave when ordered to do so. A crisis over the Black Hills was looming, especially after yet another commission showed up at the southern agencies and attempted to buy the hills in September 1875. This time Red Cloud wanted nothing to do with the negotiation, which fell mostly on the shoulders of Spotted Tail. In the final exchange of offers, the Indians demanded presents and annuities for "seven generations," a figure that the commissioners considered to be astronomical. When the commissioners countered by asking if they could lease the hills for the sum of $400,000, the Indians virtually walked out.

Although the northern tribes had been asked to join in this debate over the fate of the Black Hills, most of them remained in camps on the Tongue River throughout the summer. Some nineteen hundred lodges of Hunkpapas, Minneconjous, Sans Arcs, Cheyennes, and Oglalas now joined together to voice outrage at the invasion of the Black Hills by the *wasicuns*. When other reservation Indians talked with these people, they found the northern bands to be ready for war and committed to running the *wasicuns* out of the hills. Late that fall, a special meeting occurred in Washington to resolve the Black Hills issue.

The men who came together at the White House in November 1875 seemed convinced that the only solution to the growing crisis on the Great Plains was war. General Sherman argued that the best way to pursue the situation was to let the army take charge. He proposed to issue a decree in which all Indians living outside the reservation boundaries—obviously meaning the northern bands in the Powder and Tongue River valleys—were to report to their agencies by January 31, 1876, or they would be considered "hostile." President Grant, the author of the peace policy, reluctantly concurred with his old Civil War colleague Sherman. In effect, without provocation, the United States declared war on the Sioux.

For the Lakota people, the fall of 1875 and the spring of 1876 represented a time of trial. Many Indians—indeed the majority—had generally given up the hunt and seemed destined to remain peaceful on reservations. Large populations existed near Spotted Tail and Red Cloud Agencies, whereas others could be found at Crow Creek, Cheyenne River, and Standing Rock Agencies. However, the leaders of these reservation Indians—Red Cloud, Spotted Tail, Running Antelope, and others—had lost prestige, especially among the young men in their bands. The young men searched for new leaders who might show them how to resist the growing American encroachment on their lands. And the young men on the reservations showed signs of rebellion against the entire reservation system. They often felt cheated by their agents and, on occasion, they found that soldiers near the agencies took advantage of their women. Many had armed themselves with new weapons—repeating rifles in particular—and seemed primed for conflict.

Accordingly, as the army prepared to settle the "Sioux Problem," many a young Sioux warrior looked for new ways to remove the demanding Americans, to return the land to its former ways when the buffalo provided the needs of the people rather than the agent and his freight trains. Red Cloud had tried to rally the Sioux nation and commit it to a unified policy of negotiation, but he had clearly failed. An obvious option to Red Cloud's accommodation for many young Sioux men was to join the northern bands, whose numbers began to swell with Yanktons, Yanktonais, and even some Sissetons, Wahpetons, Wahpekutes, and Mdewakantons. These Indians turned to the chiefs of the northern tribes for leadership, including the Hunkpapa Sitting Bull.

Sitting Bull soon epitomized the spirit of Lakota and even to some degree, Sioux, nationhood. He seemed determined to rally all Sioux people against the American threat. He refused to negotiate with the *wasicuns* at any cost or to recognize their claim to land. More important, as every young Lakota warrior knew by 1875, Sitting Bull had powerful medicine. He possessed an understanding of the unknown that made him especially suited for leadership.

That fall, then, as President Grant and his generals plotted against the Sioux, the future of the Lakota people increasingly fell from the hands of the reservation chiefs into the clutches of the energetic and determined war leaders among the northern bands, the most dynamic being the Hunkpapa Sitting Bull. Although few Americans knew much of this man, he had ample experience as a leader of his people. To him, the very thought of accepting annuities at the reservations was anathema. The Great Spirit to whom he prayed never would have sanctioned an abandonment of the Lakota ways of hunting and intertribal fighting.

Thus, as the United States prepared to enter a new year, 1876, the one-hundred-year celebration of American Independence, a war on the Great Plains loomed on the horizon. The northern tribes would fight rather than be driven to dependency on the reservations. And Sitting Bull would lead them.

CHAPTER 2

Sitting Bull's Tiospaye *and the Formulation of Sioux Leadership*

❖
❖

The Hunkpapa society that Sitting Bull grew into was rich with complexity despite the rather simple economy of buffalo hunting and gathering that the western Sioux depended on. Sociopolitical structure existed on many levels, with people having a strong sense of where they fit into the society and what they could expect of their fellow tribesmen. With order and stability came loyalty and obedience to tribal norms. For the most part, Lakota boys lived in a very secure environment, grew to adulthood with a strong reverence for their elders, and when entering manhood, instinctively defended their families and their society from any outside threat.

Nevertheless, the Lakota people had been on the plains for only a generation or two, and sociopolitical formation was in a state of flux. As the decade of the 1850s drew to a close, conflict with Americans increased at the same time in which the society saw many relatives give up plains hunting for life as reservation accommodationists. These changes brought some Sioux people to rethink what it meant to be Lakota, indeed, what it meant to be part of the Lakota nation. As a young man, much of Sitting Bull's early training encompassed such issues, and in his case, these debates led to a stronger enhancement of perceived Lakota identity. He entered a state of maturity convinced that the ways of the forefather were decidedly the best for his people.

Those ancestors had lived in relative harmony by developing a series of overlapping political networks solidified by kinship relationships. A "Chiefs' Society" founded on hereditary ascendancy held sway over a council that consisted of chiefs and elders. The hereditary chiefs generally decided local political issues. War chiefs, in turn, emerged from among male societies that at times competed with the hereditary chiefs. But even the male societies competed with one another over membership and for tribal influence. Young Sitting Bull, then, was born into a society that was anything but egalitarian, but it was also a society prone to factional dispute and occasional disorder. Strong unity, or support for a national cause, could emerge in such a society only when it was faced with an overwhelming threat to its existence. Little did Sitting Bull know that such a threat would emerge over his lifetime, and he would be thrust into the role of defending Sioux nationhood.

Sioux kinship networks functioned within the framework of the *tiospaye,* or the collection of families, or lodge groups, who made up the Hunkpapa band. When winter forced the *tiospaye,* or the band, to break down into smaller groups, the *wicotipi*—or closely related kin—remained as the smallest camp unit. Sources disagree, but there were generally anywhere from four to seven Hunkpapa *wicotipis* in the last half of the nineteenth century (the changing number is reflective of increased factionalism). They held anywhere from a few to several dozen families. And within each camp group, at least one powerful family emerged with a hereditary chief, who spoke for the entire group.

Although *wicotipis* remained fluid during the best of times, with a fringe element of people coming and going, the growing pressures of American invasion increasingly affected the size and success of such groups. Nevertheless, as a young Lakota man, Sitting Bull identified himself as a member of a particular *wicotipi* within the Hunkpapa *tiospaye,* and he lived and worked within these groups for virtually his entire life.

Sitting Bull grew to maturity within one of the two most important *wicotipis* among the Hunkpapa people. His biological father was Jumping Bull, a man of considerable accomplishment as a hunter and a warrior, and his biological mother was Her Holy Door. The Lakota practiced bilocal marriage for the most part, but young men who belonged to important families seldom left them to live with their new in-laws at marriage. Jumping Bull was no exception, staying within the *wicotipi* of his two powerful brothers, Four Horns and Looks-For-Him-In-A-Tent.

These two brothers, or uncles of Sitting Bull, had sons. But the children never appear in later accounts, and they apparently never grew to maturity. This would not have mattered, for in Lakota culture, uncles raised nephews. The two brothers became the most important role models in Sitting Bull's life, teaching him the arts of hunting and warfare. But Four Horns and Looks-For-Him-In-A-Tent, along with several other key Hunkpapa leaders, also assured Sitting Bull of being seriously considered as a potential leader of his people, for the two brothers were major Hunkpapa chiefs.

Sitting Bull's uncle Four Horns served as the hereditary political chief of the *Icira-hingla wicotipi.* This term meant literally the lodge group where "everyone is always disputing one another." This position, as hereditary chief, gave Four Horns the right to wear a "hair-coat," the primary symbol of leadership among the Hunkpapa people. Looks-For-Him-In-A-Tent served as a war chief within the *wicotipi,* a position quite different from the political role played by Four Horns but nearly as powerful. Obviously, the lodge group had historically fallen victim to factionalism and division, as the name implies. Yet it appears that these brothers and their father (Sitting Bull's grandfather), also an important chief, had brought stability to the lodge group by 1830.

Within the next few decades, the brothers naturally coalesced around Sitting Bull, lessening the potential for future divisiveness. Helping in this political consolidation was yet another hereditary political chief, Black Moon. The leader of a different *wicotipi,* Black Moon was revered as a man of great spiritual power and also served as a "hair-coat wearer." Though Black Moon had three sons, all were killed at young ages, and Black Moon increasingly placed his attention on young Sitting Bull, who was his cousin. Black Moon came to support Sitting Bull in all that he did, broadening the power of the *Icira-hingla wicotipi.*

Other important Lakota warriors joined Sitting Bull's *wicotipi* as it became the center of opposition to American aggressiveness. Such men included One Bull, the son of Sitting Bull's sister by a Minneconjou chief, Makes Room. Even though the marriage never lasted very long—One Bull's mother would eventually live in Sitting Bull's tent—Sitting Bull adopted One Bull as his own son. When One Bull married, he pitched a tepee next to Sitting Bull's. This nephew and adopted son became a staunch supporter of Sitting Bull.

The marriage of Sitting Bull's sister to Makes Room produced yet another son, White Bull, who remained with his father's people, the Minneconjous. But White Bull frequently joined Sitting Bull's *tiospaye* and often fought alongside his uncle. Indeed, the marriage, which occurred about 1848, seemed to bring the most energetic leaders among the Minneconjous together with those of the Hunkpapa. Sitting Bull would receive more support from some of his Minneconjou in-laws than from certain *wicotipis* of his own *tiospaye.* Make's Room's sons, One Bull and White Bull, would also live well into the twentieth century and leave a marvelous oral history account of their famous uncle.[1]

Kinship connections had such an important impact on Hunkpapa history because competition existed among Hunkpapa *wicotipis* as well as among the various Lakota

---

[1] These oral history materials are found in the Walter Stanley Campbell Papers, Western History Collections, University of Oklahoma.

tiospayes. Jealousy reared its ugly head for a variety of reasons. Sometimes something as simple as having two men compete for the hand of the same woman caused trouble. At other times, the redistribution of material goods created schisms, jealousies erupting when annuities were handed out or when horses taken in a raid were divided up.

Sitting Bull would face such jealousy when he got older. Yet as he grew to maturity, he found himself living within a unique collection of relatives, all of whom had proper forms of address and positions in the Hunkpapa *tiospaye* and the Lakota tribe. Kinship connections, or being, as the Lakota said, "of the blood," or *owe*, provided mechanism for solving serious jealousies. They held the various *wicotipis* together so that they could form one *tiospaye*. One's relatives proved crucial in giving a person an identity and, of course, in fostering that person's aspirations of leadership.

Since Sitting Bull remained the only young male among three important Hunkpapa brothers, these men showered him with affection and attention from his early days. In turn, in standard Lakota parlance, he viewed all three of these men as his "father," and he called them *Ate*, the Lakota word for father. Biological status simply remained less important than the kinship relationship that the tribal social structure created. In other words, Sitting Bull possessed three fathers, all of whom gave him status and instruction and saw to it that he was raised properly.

Although one's relatives played key roles in defining one's position in the society, a strong bond of loyalty also developed within the circle of closest male relatives. Cousins were identified in conversation as being either *tahansi*, meaning the male cousin of a male, or *sicesi*, the male cousin of a female. Every relationship had a definition and usually a place of importance. Thus, when in the heat of battle, and a relative needed help, a warrior called that person directly by his kin name, saying, "*tahansi*, come and help me!" All Sioux men knew that they could count on their relatives in a fight or for sustenance

during times of famine. The role of kinship became so important in molding the society that when a non-Lakota stranger
faced certain death at the hands of Sioux warriors, he often
cried out in the Lakota language "cousin save me," in an often
futile attempt to convince the Lakota warriors to spare his life
through a battlefield adoption.

Sitting Bull seemed destined from the beginning to play an
important role in this society. While having many of the right
relatives to train him, he also reached the most productive
years of his life during a period of trial and transition, during a
period when American invasion prompted the various Lakota
bands to put more of an effort into political centralization. And
he nurtured that most important trait that could not be learned
or even purchased from a medicine man. He discovered very
early that he possessed a unique relationship with the *Wakantanka,* or the Great Spirit. Others within his band and nation
soon came to recognize this power. He would have many visions in his life, and all of them came true. His people came to
know this.

The visions that Sitting Bull would one day use to guide
his people came from a learning process that began in earnest
when a young Sioux boy first learned to walk. Stories of bravery and sacrifice filled the air inside the tepee nearly every
evening after dark. Such stories often centered on past relatives who had helped save the people by doing something
brave. The sense of dedication and loyalty bestowed by such
folklore on the young made them eager to take a place in the
society as a provider and protector.

The serious training of a young boy began after he was
able to mount a horse. Horses had special meaning to the
Sioux people, for they were foremost buffalo hunters who depended on the horse to follow the migrating herds. Buffalo
ribs and steaks fed the people, and buffalo hides provided
winter jackets and skins for tepee construction. Indeed, the
dating of the Lakota movement west of the Missouri River is
directly tied to their acquisition of the horse, which occurred

about 1750. Thanks to the reminiscences of Sitting Bull's nephews One Bull and White Bull, who both experienced boyhood in Hunkpapa and Minneconjou camps during the 1850s, we know much about this early learning experience.

Boys, such as young Sitting Bull, received instructions in tending horse herds at the age of six. They rose at dawn and moved the animals from the village, which they always located in a river valley, to better grass several miles from the camp center. By noon, they drove them back to water and completed the cycle one more time before dark. During winter, the process had added chores, since often the boys had to tear down supple cottonwood branches for the animals to munch on. In order to handle such responsibilities, *ates* first taught the boys how to ride, starting with gentle horses and working upward to wild animals newly captured on the plains, instructing them to hang onto the mane of the animal while being tossed from side to side. By the time a boy reached ten years of age, he could generally handle any horse in camp and usually owned one or two of his own.

The next step in the training process involved teaching the youngster how to train horses to act under the stresses of buffalo hunting—which meant teaching them to run at a full gallop alongside the buffalo without getting gored—and during combat. Boys plunged their horses into rapidly running streams, even during winter, and learned how to swim with the current. They rode the animal hard, teaching it to turn in a flash in order to avert trouble. Young Sioux boys literally lived with their favorite horse and came to know it so well that they commonly talked with their animals. Sitting Bull was no different. He spoke with his favorite war horse all the time, and most observers concluded that the animal fully understood him.

The final test of riding skills came in learning how to fire a weapon accurately from a fast-moving horse. Sioux boys worked first with bows and arrows and lances, freeing their hands to work the weapons and staying on their horse while using only the pressure exerted by their legs. General Anson Mills, who left an account of the Battle of the Rosebud in 1876, thought Sioux warriors to be the most astonishing cavalry he had ever seen. "In charging up towards us," he wrote, "they exposed little of their person, hanging on with one arm around the neck and one leg over the horse, firing and lancing from underneath the horses neck." The American cavalry troops saw very little to fire at, and most frequently they downed an Indian by killing his horse. This often led to exaggerated reports of the numbers of Indians killed in any one engagement. Of course, young men became even more effective as warriors once they replaced the bows and arrows with high caliber rifles.

But the training of Sitting Bull went beyond simply learning how to handle horses. In the process of preparing the Lakota young man for the hunt and war, boys had mock battles in which they learned just how their horses would respond during certain circumstances. A classic trick included riding war horses through heavy brush areas while a single boy hid with a musket and fired the weapon at an appropriate time. Boys repeated this until the animal got used to hearing close sounds of gunfire. Such exercises eventually brought boy and animal to the point where either could anticipate what the other would do, and the practice made Sioux warriors some of the most successful cavalry in the world. In the heat of battle, the Indian ponies seldom if ever shied or bolted at the noise of gunfire, and they often came when the warrior called them.

Sitting Bull had mastered this training scenario by 1845, the approximate year of his fourteenth birthday. This allowed him to accompany the men on a buffalo hunt, such an event marking the entry of a boy into manhood. All young Sioux lads took this responsibility with considerable seriousness. Indeed, when they mounted their hunting horse and sought out the herds, most undoubtedly wondered whether they and the animal they rode were prepared. Sitting Bull's teachers dressed him appropriately for the event as he left camp clad only in a breechcloth, with his hair braided and tied back. His *ates* carefully painted both the youth and his horse the sacred color of red, signifying life, covering appropriate parts of the animals legs and head and Sitting Bull's arms, forehead, and legs. With such guiding support, Sitting Bull became one of the best hunters among the Hunkpapa people. On one hunt, White Bull saw him completely drive arrows through the necks of two buffalos in one afternoon. Such success was unusual, but it became common for Sitting Bull to kill three or four animals in a day's hunt, bringing back to the village an excess of meat.

Part of the reason for his success at hunting came from his knowledge of animals, an obviously learned trait, and the spiritual relationship that he possessed with them. He spoke with animals on many occasions, carrying on dialogues with buffalos, meadowlarks, and wolves. One story, perhaps apocryphal, suggests that he obtained his name after a brief encounter with a buffalo. White Bull related that when Sitting Bull was just six years old and still known by his childhood name, *Hunkesni*, or Slow, he met a large buffalo bull while out tending horses. Reaching the crest of a hill, he saw the bull sitting on his haunches, and "the bull was looking at him in such a manner that he could not break away from it." But the animal showed no signs of anger and simply turned away, saying as he left, "Sitting Bull you've pitied me—thank you—I respect you."

When home, Sitting Bull told his father of this unusual experience, and he called the medicine men of the *tiospaye* to hear the tale. They all agreed that this omen meant that Sitting Bull would always be successful in the hunt. They concluded that the buffalo, having a mind of his own, felt that Sitting Bull had honored him and thus all buffalos. Thereafter, the animals would always allow Sitting Bull to kill them for food. Such permission, though, demanded sacrifice and the occasional levying of a prayer to the buffalo, something that Sitting Bull never forgot. On hearing the rendition of the medicine men, Jumping Bull promptly called the camp crier into the lodge, gave him a present, and told him to announce to the people that his son would have a new name—Sitting Bull.[2]

On another occasion, Sitting Bull met with a wolf while on a hunt. Again, he seemed to sense that the wolf had no intention of harming him but instead wished to give him advice. As Sitting Bull listened, the wolf said, "Friend, I am living on this earth and am having a hard time. Everything I go after . . . sometimes I get it and sometimes I don't." Then, he continued in a sorrowful tone, "My life is a hard life and you will have to take after me." As the wolf drifted off into the distance, Sitting Bull could hear the refrains of a song that the animal sang: "How come my life is harder than other animals?"

Again, Sitting Bull returned to his people to discover what this meant. The medicine men finally concluded that though Sitting Bull would have a difficult and even lonely life like the wolf, he would always find something to eat. Of course, the medicine men agreed that however difficult his search for sustenance, Sitting Bull should share this food with his people. Stories, songs, and oral history, then, tied the society together, seniors to juniors, and provided an honored place for elders who saw their calling as one of interpreting such accounts.

Given this knowledge, Sitting Bull came to respect the wisdom that the animals gave to him. Although such encounters forced him to seek advice from elders who interpreted the messages, this gave these men status in a society that placed considerable emphasis on warfare and hunting, jobs generally relegated to the young. The ties that Sitting Bull developed with animals unquestionably affected his development as a leader. After encountering the wolf, he often went off alone to hunt, almost always returning to the village with game. Later in life, when being pressed by the army, Sitting Bull would

---

[2]Another story recorded in the 1930s suggests that Jumping Bull gave Sitting Bull his name after his return from a successful raid in which he killed a Crow Indian.

first look to the old and the sick and find a place of refuge for them. His success as a hunter led to greater appreciation of the spiritual world from which that success came.

Jumping Bull frequently exploited this success by hiring a herald to announce to the camp the results of Sitting Bull's hunt. And Sitting Bull consistently gave away the majority of his meat to feed large numbers of people. He particularly sought out the elderly and the sick and obtained a reputation as the most generous man among his people. They, in turn, blessed him and sang his praise. Such generosity was not uncommon, since everyone helped their own relatives, but some young hunters believed that the old, the poor, and especially unwanted widows were useless and should be left to fend for themselves. Sitting Bull helped them and others. Indeed, he even killed a buffalo on one occasion in order to give the majority of the carcass to a young wolf that had been following him. He was an extremely generous man in a society that made generosity the ultimate virtue.

Feeding the people constituted important service, but every young Sioux boy yearned for the chance to demonstrate valor in defense of the society. Sitting Bull was no different. The Sioux did glorify war, but they sent their young men off to fight for two specific reasons. They had to maintain control over migrating animal herds, and this meant running off other competitors, and they needed to mount raids in order to obtain horses so that they could reach and exploit these herds.

The theft of horses became essential since many mounts perished over the winter. Often the Sioux hunter gave up trying to protect all of his horses when severe blizzards descended on the northern plains, trying only to save the two or three best ones. Raiding, then, occurred on a large scale, the Hunkpapa fighting almost continuously with the Crow Indians for horses as well as for the rich buffalo lands of the Powder River valley, and even with the distant Flatheads of the Rocky Mountains and the Assiniboins, from the lands north of the Missouri River.

The Hunkpapa concentrated most of their raiding activity in the west where every year they clashed with the Crows. These fights generally resulted in few casualties, but they went on because both people realized that the Powder and Bighorn River valleys possessed some of the largest buffalo herds in America. These animals became essential for the Sioux if they were to maintain their way of life. As Sitting Bull reached his fourteenth year, he applied to the leaders of one of the male societies to be included in a party that sought Crow horses. As he prepared for departure, his *ates* and his mother made him special gifts.

The gifts given to Sitting Bull were the sort that all parents wish to give their children when they reach adulthood—presents designed to facilitate the transition to successful warriorhood. The first item was a lance, complete with notches on the blade and a feather on the end. Usually made from a discarded sword, the lance had to be blessed by a medicine man before being used. A more elegant gift came next—a sacred shield. The shield had special meaning since parents purchased information from a medicine man on what kinds of figures to draw on it. The shield given to Sitting Bull had a blue-green color underlay with sky and clouds in the background. The figure of a man with winglike arms dominated the center, the figure symbolizing heaven and earth. This man had four feathers on his head, and tufts of hair hung from various spots, the latter being the symbol of power. Once assuming such a sacred shield, the owner had to tell the truth and to never think bad thoughts. To break the taboo, meant death!

Although the *ates* fretted, Sitting Bull's training readied him for this dangerous trial, and the fathers knew that he must go. They simply wanted to make him as prepared as possible for the task ahead. For transportation, Jumping Bull gave Sitting Bull his best war horse, a sturdy gray animal, no doubt a horse that Sitting Bull had trained on for many years. Besides the blessed lance and shield, Sitting Bull also carried a bow and arrows. Black Moon and Four Horns made these, both men being reputed to be excellent arrow makers. Finally, Sitting Bull's armament included a metal hatchet, no doubt purchased by one of the *ates* at some trade store along the Missouri River.

The party of ten sullen men that Sitting Bull joined rode hard into the west, taking but a few days to reach the lands disputed with the Crow. As they crossed a divide somewhere beyond the Powder River, suddenly a dozen Crows appeared in front of them. Each man fought for himself in these engagements, but he did so knowing that a Sioux warrior would never desert a comrade and would take the most outlandish risks to retrieve a fallen relative. With this in mind, Sitting Bull lurched ahead, challenging an individual Crow in combat. The adversary turned to run at the sight of the hatchet-wielding Sitting Bull, but the sturdy gray horse gained on the Crow. As Sitting Bull came alongside his quarry, he struck a vicious blow to the head of the Crow, knocking him to the ground. Whether the enemy was unconscious or dead mattered not to the Sioux, Sitting Bull had counted first "coup," and he watched as his fellow warriors came on and took the scalp of the helpless Crow, one of seven or eight taken that day.[3]

Both White Bull and One Bull remembered distinctly this story of bravery, for it gave Sitting Bull the right to wear a lone eagle feather, the Sioux ribbon for valor. Seldom if ever did a Sioux warrior at the age of fourteen count first coup in a battle. As soon as Sitting Bull reached camp, Jumping Bull hired a crier to announce his success, reaffirming once again that all should now call the young man Sitting Bull. Jumping Bull then gave a large feast in which all the *ates* and other relatives came.

---

[3]The Sioux called counting coup *aopazan*. This did not necessarily mean killing an opponent but rather striking him on the head with either a bow, hatchet, or coup stick. This was literally the bravest thing a warrior could do. Once down, other men could follow and count second and even third coup.

Finally, Jumping Bull gave away a horse to further publicize the deed. Sitting Bull had successfully entered manhood.

The story of this first coup soon became one of many that would follow. The very next year, 1846, Sitting Bull again found himself in a battle, this time with the more heavily armed Flathead Indians from the Rocky Mountains. "He dashed in along the Flathead lines," White Bull reported, in an act designed specifically to demonstrate bravery. As the Flatheads fired their muzzle-loaded guns at Sitting Bull, he felt a sharp pain in the foot. This wound gave Sitting Bull the right to wear a red-tipped feather in his head, after being wounded in battle.

As the years passed, Sitting Bull fought in more skirmishes, especially with the Crows. Some of the oral history accounts of this activity collected in the 1930s almost defy believability. Yet in later years, Sitting Bull would depict himself in ledger art with thirty coup feathers, an obvious indication of the truth of the accounts. Perhaps the most stirring involved Sitting Bull's challenge to a single Crow warrior, who on searching his quiver, found that he had no arrows. Sitting Bull, with three remaining, fired two in the dirt near his opponent to give the man a chance, and then the Hunkpapa killed the Crow with the remaining one.

Yet another example of Sitting Bull's single combat with a Crow came after the adversaries withdrew from battle. A lone chief replete in headdress and brilliant garb returned to challenge whoever among the Sioux dared fight him. Sitting Bull responded. In classic fashion, reminiscent of a joust in the Middle Ages, both men came straight at each other, their horses at a dead run. Leveling muskets, both fired almost instantaneously. The Crow chief fell from his horse, shot through the stomach. But Sitting Bull also suffered a wound, a bullet striking his foot just underneath the toes and traveling the length of his entire foot. The ball exited at the heel, but the wound never healed properly, and Sitting Bull severely limped the rest of his life.

Undoubtedly, Sitting Bull's most serious wound came in fighting the Americans. In the aftermath of the running fight with General Sully near the Killdeer Mountains, Sitting Bull led a charge against "Captain" James L. Fisk's wagon train of miners and took a bullet in the left hip. The lead then moved up the bone and lodged in the small of his back. Since many men received wounds that day, Sitting Bull asked for no special help, even riding the seven miles back to camp unassisted.

All this success in battle led to many honors. In all, Sitting Bull earned the right to wear thirty feathers in his headdress, each one representing a coup or a touching of an enemy. He also could mark the right shoulder of his buckskin shirt with an X, signifying that he had been wounded while killing an enemy in battle. Although a few men would count more coups than Sitting Bull, no one could possibly question the bravery of this man. In the last decade of Sitting Bull's life, observers noted a number of scars and a physical debilitation, clearly the consequences of his many combats.

Yet honors in war came with a price for the Lakota people. As Sitting Bull reached middle age, he saw many of his close friends and relatives die in intertribal fights. In every Lakota camp, there were always many more women than men as a result of war. The first serious loss for Sitting Bull came in 1859 when Crows surprised his *wicotipi* and killed two herd boys. All the warriors sprang to their horses and, with Jumping Bull in the lead, went in hot pursuit. Now a man well past the prime of life, Jumping Bull reportedly had suffered a terrible toothache the night before and wished to die. He sought out a lone Crow, and the younger opponent stabbed Jumping Bull to death with a sword. Sitting Bull arrived too late to save him and went on a rampage, killing five Crows thereafter. When other Crow captives were brought in, everyone expected Sitting Bull to take out his sorrow by having them killed as well. Instead, he asked that they be let go, saying in a subdued tone, "My father is a man and death is his."

About ten years later, Sitting Bull's uncle Looks-For-Him-In-a-Tent also died at the hands of Crows. This battle occurred in the open flats north of the Missouri River when the Hunkpapas discovered thirty well-armed but unmounted Crows who, sensing their ultimate fate, dug into the top of a hill. The Hunkpapas sent in over a hundred men but lost fourteen before completely destroying the Crows, a huge loss for both sides. The deaths of Sitting Bull's father and uncle had an impact on him. By the latter 1860s, most every oral history account of his life suggests that he held back in battle, letting the younger men take the brunt of the fighting. Of course, he was nearly forty years old by this time and beyond the prime age for fighting.

But Sitting Bull's decision to act more cautiously probably originated as well from a growing familial responsibility. Although American observers at the close of the nineteenth century would contend that Sitting Bull never really fought at the major battles with American troops, which with the exception of Killdeer Mountain, in fact was true, they failed to understand that given Sitting Bull's station and the large number of people in his family, it was not expected that he go into combat in later years. He had taken several wives by this time, and he supported various children, as well as an aged mother. Very likely the wives and mother both cautioned him to take care of himself rather than take the risks that young men normally took.

Sitting Bull's venture into matrimony occurred for the first time during the early 1850s when he married a woman named Light Hair. He would marry eight other times in the next twenty years, some of these unions lasting for only a short time. Lakota marriage offered a young man the opportunity to align himself with certain powerful kinship groups. For any man with political ambition, marriage became a way in which allies could be recruited. Certainly, Sitting Bull viewed marriage as beneficial both for the companionship that it offered and for the chance that it provided to expand the influence of his *wicotipi.*

The Lakota had extremely flexible rules on marriage that allowed men to go live wherever they wished. The only real regulation was that a man not marry a woman from his own *wicotipi*, or immediate lodge group. Such a union would have constituted incest. As far as where the newlyweds would live, the Lakota generally followed bilocal rules, allowing the man to move in with his new wife's relatives when that suited the arrangement, or vice-versa. But when a man came from a powerful family, such as Sitting Bull, most young men preferred to stay with their male relatives and they found wives who would move in with them. Indeed, Sitting Bull's wives came to live with him, and virtually all of Sitting Bull's male relatives took wives back to their *wicotipi*.[4] To some degree, this explains why the kin group associated with Sitting Bull became so powerful by the 1870s.

Yet Sitting Bull had hard luck in marriage, with many unions failing for one reason or another. Light Hair eventually fought with Sitting Bull's second wife, Snow On Her, causing such discord in the camp that both women ultimately left. When Sitting Bull finally did find a more suitable union, the woman died from an epidemic in 1869, along with at least one of Sitting Bull's children. A year later, he married the sisters of a relatively important Hunkpapa warrior from another *wicotipi*, named Gray Eagle who moved in with Sitting Bull's *wicotipi*, a clear indication of his rising status and influence. This last dual marriage which lasted until Sitting Bull's death, turned out to be quite beneficial for Sitting Bull since Gray Eagle became a staunch supporter of the rising chief and brought many of his relatives along when the plains wars reached their peak. These two women bore Sitting Bull four children, one a boy whom he named Crowfoot.

---

[4]When matrilocal marriage occurred, the father of the bride often had a special tepee set up on the edge of the camp, called in Lakota a *tiotipi*, in which he made a place for his new son-in-law, the idea being to gradually introduce the man to his new *wicotipi* and, thus, his new relatives.

Sitting Bull needed to be cautious in war, given his new familial responsibilities, but he also grew up in a family in which he had no full brothers. Should Sitting Bull have been killed, his children would have lacked *ates* to train them. This clearly bothered the future Lakota leader. An unusual chance to change this situation, however, came during the winter of 1857-1858, when the Hunkpapas had a scrape with the Assiniboins. Sitting Bull and several other warriors came on an Assiniboin family, most of whom they killed. The only remaining member was a young boy of about ten or eleven, who kept the Sioux at bay until his last arrow had been fired. Once this happened, the Lakota rushed in and were about to kill the brave child when the young Assiniboin faced Sitting Bull and called out in the Siouan language, "Big Brother, save me."

Startled, Sitting Bull promptly placed himself between the vengeful warriors and the boy and announced that he intended to adopt this *Hohe,* or Assiniboin child. Very small children could be adopted with some certainty of success, but the men present argued against the idea. The boy had defended himself quite well, and they feared bringing such a lad into camp. But Sitting Bull refused to let them have him and, once back at his lodge, the chief proceeded to initiate an elaborate adoption ceremony. In effect, the ceremony made the young man an affine kin, giving him relatives and a Lakota name, Stays Back.

To convince his fellow tribesmen of the adoption, Sitting Bull gave presents to those who seemed most opposed, and he offered them the peace pipe to obtain their consent. To introduce the young man to the band, he threw a large feast in which everyone came to eat with their new Hunkpapa relative. The young Assiniboin lived up to the honor that Sitting Bull had bestowed on him by becoming a loyal supporter, fulfilling the role of brother in Sitting Bull's lodge. To further consummate this relationship, when the young Assiniboin successfully went through the trial of manhood, Sitting Bull rewarded him by giving him his father's name of Jumping Bull. Sitting Bull's adopted brother would remain loyal to the end, dying in defense of his brother Sitting Bull when Indian police tried to arrest him in 1890.

The success with Jumping Bull prompted Sitting Bull to attempt one other adoption, which had a far less satisfactory ending. In January 1869, while on a raiding party, warriors from Sitting Bull's village captured a nineteen-year-old mail rider named Frank Grouard. Just as two Sioux warriors were about to kill him, Sitting Bull appeared and knocked one of them down. The other scurried off as Sitting Bull motioned to Grouard to sit down and smoke. Afterward, Sitting Bull took the young man back to camp and asked the Chiefs' Society for permission to keep and adopt him as yet another brother. After some debate, the elders agreed. Sitting Bull went to Grouard and explained his new position, telling him "these are my relatives and you are to call them as I do. Just treat them fair, and you will get along with them." But others in camp opposed the adoption, for Grouard was a man and he was the enemy, and for over a year, Sitting Bull and his followers kept watch over Grouard, fearful that an opponent would kill him.

Unlike Jumping Bull, Grouard failed to assimilate and waited for his chance to escape. This opportunity came in 1873 when Grouard fled to the reservations and promptly took a job as a guide for the army. He helped lead troops into the Powder River country over the winter of 1876 and later in the year led the army to the Sioux at Slim Buttes. Sitting Bull could not understand such disloyalty, especially after he had saved Grouard's life. "One time that man should have been killed," he confided to White Bull. "I kept him and now he has joined the soldiers."

Although it took Sitting Bull nearly two decades to produce a stable married life and he had only mixed results at adopting relatives, his growing reputation as a spiritual man took shape nearly from childhood. As his nephew later said, Sitting Bull quickly attained a reputation as a *wicasa wakan,* which meant that he had the unique ability to see things, to understand the past or predict the future through dreams, and visions. As a youth, he often had dreams and his parents hired the most respected holy men in the band to interpret them. These elders came to see that Sitting Bull had a special relationship with the mystery power, with *Wakantanka*.

The special power that Sitting Bull possessed derived in part from his ties with animals. Lakotas viewed animals on much the same level as human beings, with several exceptions—some animals had the unique power to transform themselves into something else, for good and bad purposes, and others, became messengers, or harbingers of good and evil. The most successful *wicasa wakans* had close relationships with various animals, talking with them regularly. Sitting Bull developed unique ties with the buffalo, the meadowlark, and the wolf. Hunkpapa holy men respected such knowledge, even when it came from a young boy, and when Sitting Bull became a young adult, his power only enhanced his leadership ability.

Such power had to be nurtured, however, since often young men had encounters and dreams and nothing became of them. Sitting Bull again turned to his relatives for help in this training, approaching Black Moon and Four Horns, two well-known *wicasa wakans*. They had acquired a mastery of the natural world that allowed them insight into the sacred world of the great mystery, the *Wakantanka*. Sitting Bull's training, which would enable him to follow in their footsteps, included instruction on how to pray to *Wakantanka*, had to seek visions, how to cleanse the soul in the sweet bath, and how to understand the mystery of the sacred stones. Sitting Bull, on entering adulthood, became one of the most religious young men in the Hunkpapa *tiospaye*, and he was ready for his great test giving sacrifice to *Wakantanka* in the sun dance ceremony.

Just when Sitting Bull participated in his first sun dance is not clear. White Bull, who left an account, was too young to remember the date. It obviously occurred in the 1850s, or just after Sitting Bull had reached his twentieth birthday. As White Bull described it, Sitting Bull begged of the Great Spirit to allow him success while on a hunt. He got down from his horse, filled his pipe, and lit it. He held the pipe up in front of him, bowl toward him and stem upright, right hand on the bowl and left hand on the stem. And he prayed: "*Wakantanka* please help me & save me & pull me through all troubles. I'll give you some buffalo hides & some tobacco & some of my flesh." The promise having been made and the hunt being successful, Sitting Bull then returned to his camp to ask the holy men for permission to dance in the next sun dance.

This ceremony, the most significant religious ritual performed among the Lakota people, occurred every June when the various *wicotipis* came together to form one large village. It was a joyous time when young people courted and children played games in large groups. The festival celebrated the coming of summer and the good times that came with it. But it also had its serious side, for a religious fervor overtook the people. As it did, selected men went forward to give sacrifice for gifts given by the *Wakantanka* over the past year. In this atmosphere, the dancers came together—often anywhere from ten to forty in number—and placed themselves under the direction of the head holy man of the village who directed the ritual. During the 1850s, the Hunkpapa Dreamer-of-the-Sun held this honor, but after his death the duty often fell to Black Moon.

The head *wicasa wakan* acted as the master of ceremonies, and other lesser shamans assisted him. They first instructed the novices on how to behave, telling them never to steal from their Lakota kinsmen, nor to lie. They pointed out that the Great Spirit, whose aid they sought, always watched them. After instruction, the young men went to a nearby river, and with the help of a young female virgin, cut down a long cottonwood pole. They brought it to camp and placed it upright in a hole, securing smaller stakes in a circle surrounding the pole, weaving willows between the stakes, and thereby making a dance arena. With a large crowd of mostly women and children looking on from outside the enclosure, the opening ceremonies began as the morning sun reached a reasonable height in the eastern sky.

The dancers came into the arena dressed in buffalo robes, with only a G-string underneath. They had been fasting since the previous day to purify themselves. Other *wicasa wakans* who assisted in the dance painted them red, yellow, and black, and selected out the ones among the dancers who wished to seek an ultimate vision by having their breasts pierced. These honored men—usually anywhere from one to four—were placed on the ground, and a *wicasa wakan* pulled up a tuft of skin on either side of the heart. He then cut two gashes on either side of the tuft, inserting a cherry wood peg completely through the slits. The assistants then attached buffalo hair ropes to each stick, and they, in turn, were tied to the top of the pole, allowing the dancer to stand and stretch backward without falling.

Once done, the head *wicasa wakan* offered a prayer, and the dance began. The prayer offered at Sitting Bull's dance undoubtedly followed the usual form. The *wicasa wakan* said simply: "*Wakantanka* have mercy on me, let the tribe live long and let us have lots of buffalo." Then to the beat of a constant drum, the dancers circled the pole, dancing into the night and into the morning sun. At intervals, the dance stopped, and individuals restated why they wished to dance, some telling of successful war endeavors, success that they attributed to *Wakantanka*. At dawn, those dancers who were tethered at the breast, now tired and hungry, began to stare into the sun, hour after hour, tearing at the rope that bound them, producing excruciating pain. They continued to pray and asked for help from the Great Spirit.

Ultimately, after one or two full days, the dancer either tore away from the tethers or collapsed. Other dancers in the circle began to wither and occasionally collapsed. The head *wicasa wakan* often assisted by appearing in front of the men with a stick that had an eagle feather attached to the end. In a quick motion, he would wave the feather in front of a selected dancer, and the dancer would fall to the ground. It was during these late moments in the dance, with men strewn on the ground, that visions came.

The oral history suggests that Sitting Bull perforated his breasts and danced around the pole only once in his life. That was certainly enough. But he did participate in other sun dances, being included often in the group of thirty or forty dancers. In fact, he seemed to have danced more with age. On at least one occasion, rather than tethering himself to the pole, he sat with his back against the center pole and offered pieces of skin to *Wakantanka*. The adopted brother Jumping Bull cut the pieces from his flesh, fifty from each arm. He did this with an awl and a sharp knife, cutting small pieces of skin away from the arm the size of a match head. During the long process, which produced a great amount of blood, Sitting Bull sat completely motionless, praying.

Besides seeing visions, Sitting Bull possessed other important power that people in his society recognized and revered. He was known far and wide for the sacred *wotawe,* or medicine bag, that he possessed.[5] This power had use primarily in war, the charm being designed especially to protect the user against his enemies. One Bull later received the *wotawe* at Sitting Bull's death and revealed its content. It contained a small white stone, human hair rolled into little balls, and bits of wood and shell. This charm gave Sitting Bull special influence in leading war parties, and most young men felt honored just to be with him on such occasions. They also knew that his charm would protect them.

One Bull, on acquiring the charm, noted that Sitting Bull called on it on other occasions. For example, he controlled the weather with it, "bringing storms of wind and rain at will." Often, he would see other things of importance in the clouds that these storms brought. Despite such awesome power, Sit-

---

[5]The medicine bag, filled with certain charms, was kept near the place of honor in the tepee. Some Lakota families also had a sacred stone that served as a charm. They wrapped it in leather and kept it available in the lodge, placing it around the neck of a child when sick.

ting Bull knew that he had to respect the charm. As One Bull pointed out, if the user became "reckless," such as sending men to their death in war, "the charm would cease to have any effect." Accordingly, Sitting Bull gained a reputation as a cautious man in war, and raiding parties never suffered severe defeats while under his tutelage, making many skeptical warriors great believers.

Given Sitting Bull's sacred power, other Hunkpapas often approached him with intriguing questions. On one occasion, a man named Black Bird discovered that someone had killed his favorite horse, and in desperation he turned to Sitting Bull for help. Even though Sitting Bull was not a medicine man who sold his power, he agreed to help the man by having him partake in a sacred stone sweat bath. After entering the sweat lodge, Sitting Bull offered a prayer and sang sacred stone songs. After a time, Sitting Bull announced that the man who had perpetrated the deed would soon have a serious accident in front of Black Bird's lodge. Several days later, as young men broke horses in camp, a wild one bolted. The horse threw its rider in front of Black Bird's tepee, and the accident crushed him. Everyone then knew who had killed Black Bird's horse.

As a young man, then, Sitting Bull came to understand how his power could help his people. He sought the proper advice from other *wicasa wakans,* and he became respected as a man of knowledge, ability, and generosity. His exploits as a hunter and warrior had impressed everyone in his *tiospaye,* and he seemed destined to fulfill a major role as a leader in his society. Yet he possessed no immediate connections to a hereditary chieftainship, and it was not necessarily true that he would assume such a position even after his uncle, Four Horns, died. Young men who aspired to become chiefs, or leaders, simply did not sit at the Chiefs' Society council. This society had its own badges of authority, including the specially made "hair-coat."

Among the Hunkpapa, hereditary chiefs, or hair-coat wearers, held their positions until death. Originally, each *wicotipi* had one, the total number probably being seven. But by the 1860s, divisions and losses in war had already begun to take a toll, and four men stand out as the most dominant hair-coat wearers—Four Horns, Red Horns, Running Antelope, and Loud Voiced Hawk. Black Moon inherited a coat somewhat later, very likely from one of the other three increasingly ineffective *wicotipis*. When the *tiospayes* came together, these men, their named successors, and a few esteemed elders sat in the Chiefs' Society council chambers and debated the pressing issues that came before the band. When separated during the winter into small *wicotipis*, the individual hereditary chiefs sought advice from other elders and made unilateral decisions.

Yet the Lakota people had the foresight to separate the decision-making abilities of the hair-coat wearers from that of the executive. Hereditary chiefs never demanded anything of their people, thus their people respected them. Instead, they called on the leadership of various men's societies to carry out their advice. Sitting Bull, then, faced with the reality of never being a hair-coat wearer, yet possessing obvious skills as a leader, took a different approach to obtaining political power. He turned to the various male societies that played such a major role in Lakota life and sought leadership roles within them. Again, his uncles and his father made this rise come more easily for him.

Male societies existed among virtually all plains societies, some becoming crucially important in the development of power among village groups and others playing only minor roles. Among the seven Lakota bands, some societies included men from various *wicotipis*, and others even collected members from a cross section of the various *tiospayes*, or bands. Some societies remained small, collections of men who had something in common and wished to smoke, feast, and hunt together. Other societies remained much larger, having "chapters," for lack of a better term, in every band. Probably the most widespread male society among the Sioux was that of the Fox Society. Fox Society members could enter almost any

Sioux village on the plains, eastern or western, and find members to commune with. While all societies had various ceremonies, songs, and rules, the more prestigious the society, the more status and influence a man acquired in being asked to join it.

Sitting Bull received his first invitation to join a society at about the age of nine when the Strong Hearts asked him to become a member of their young mens' organization.[6] This boy's society emulated the adult group, learning the songs appropriate to the society and helping with feasts. When Sitting Bull went on his first buffalo hunt, at age fourteen, he joined the circle of men who belonged to the male component of the society. This likely occurred during the sun dance in June since it was common to induct new members into the society at this time of year. According to White Bull, when Sitting Bull killed the Crow with one arrow in the 1850s, the Strong Hearts made him "chief" of the society.

The induction ceremony for the Strong Hearts apparently occurred on Grand River in 1857. The elders, which included Sitting Bull's *ates,* offered him the peace pipe, gave him some water to drink, and then dipped sweet grass into the water and asked him to suck it. They then presented Sitting Bull with a large war bonnet. The war bonnet had two horns in the front, signifying that Sitting Bull was now a *blotaunka,* or war chief, and that he could lead society members, or others who wished to follow him, on war or raiding parties. But the Strong Hearts also acted on occasions as the soldier's lodge, policing the *wicotipi* over the winter, helping to organize hunts, and sending out raiding parties.

Blotaunkas generally acted as catalysts to the formation of raiding parties, often staying near the society's tepee in the

---

[6]Some evidence suggests that the Strong Hearts were created in response to early Catholic missionary efforts to form societies that would do good rather than evil and rectify wrongs.

center of camp. Thus, they were quick to lead men in battle, when the village faced a threat. When General Alfred Sully unexpectedly invaded the badlands of North Dakota in 1864, Sitting Bull took his position at the head of his relatives, including Four Horns, and as a *blotaunka* led them in battle. Yet his role was only that of a minor war chief, and most Indian informants claim that the Dakota refugee Inkpaduta directed much of the fight against the Americans. Minor war chiefs—such as Sitting Bull in 1864—did take chances in battle, however, explaining the chief's terrible wound at the hands of Fisk's party of miners that September.

As the various *tiospayes* and *wicotipis* broke up that fall of 1864, the lodges that stayed with Sitting Bull's immediate family fell back under the control of the hereditary chief, Four Horns, and the elders whom he invited to his "chiefs'" society council. But the elders did have to pick a society to implement the orders that they made in the camp. The society would then select young men to serve as "soldiers," or *akicitas,* a word that corresponds with police. The soldiers built a lodge in the center of camp, often ate together, and worked the various scouting shifts that gave security to the camp. During this particular fall, the chief's society chose the Strong Hearts, an honor for Sitting Bull since he then served as the chief soldier of the camp.

But the position had its thorny sides since that fall a Hunkpapa named Brings Plenty, brought back to the village a young white girl named Fanny Kelly. She had been taken captive along the Platte River some months before and had been traded north. Sitting Bull felt sorry for the young girl, and in his capacity as chief of the soldiers' lodge, he concluded to do something for her. He commanded Brings Plenty to send her to the Strong Hearts' lodge, an order that probably fell outside the province of the soldiers' lodge. At first, Brings Plenty refused, challenging Sitting Bull's authority. Finally, Sitting Bull went himself with several of his soldiers and placed her under the protection of the lodge. He eventually sent her to Fort Sully. "She is out of our way," the *blotaunka* said to his soldiers, "I can see in her face [that] she is homesick so I sent her back."

Other *blotaunkas* served Hunkpapa villages, and the Chiefs' Society did not always select the Strong Hearts to serve as soldiers. When given such responsibility by the hereditary chiefs, the leaders of the various soldier societies carried out orders as best as possible. Their main responsibilities included security, as well as making sure the camp had food. They always took a major role in conducting buffalo hunts, organizing the hunters, and making sure that none of them went off ahead of the main party and spooked the herd.

When some young man did sneak ahead, or break any rule, the lodge had the right to "soldier kill" that individual. Generally, that meant destroying the man's tepee and all of his goods. If the most famous man in camp did something wrong, a crisis could ensue since he obviously had plenty of relatives who would support him. Often, the soldiers simply confronted him. If the offender said, "I am a Crow," an obvious way of temporarily disavowing his kinsmen, then the soldiers could usually give him lenient punishment. However, if the man responded by saying "Friends, I am soldier like you," then the soldiers had to either back off or prepare for a serious confrontation.

On at least one occasion, Sitting Bull defied the soldiers of another lodge who came to punish him. While he was resting in his lodge with his friend, Crow King, *akicitas* confronted him. White Bull, seeing trouble, came immediately, telling his uncle Sitting Bull that he would fight with him to the death. The soldiers, leery of taking on such a threesome, wisely concluded to delay the punishment and went back to their lodge. Soldiers' lodges, then, occasionally competed for the right to police the camp, and at times, clashes occurred over their authority, producing political division that often broke along kinship lines. But the chiefs' Society tried to pick the group that the people respected most, giving considerable thought to what leaders would be placed at the head of the soldiers when they went about their duties.

Sitting Bull again showed considerable restraint and humility in executing the office of chief soldier. He always sought the proper permission when leading a party against the

Crows, and their is no record of him clashing violently with his fellow tribesmen over village rules. This honorary position of chief soldier also allowed Sitting Bull to be in total command of a party and to select scouts. In a few years, he gained a reputation of being very successful on raids, primarily because he took no foolish chances. He often broke off a fight that seemed futile, bringing his war party home unscathed.

Lakota leaders expected young warriors to be brash and to take chances, but the society did not condone the loss of large numbers of men in war. *Blotaunkas* had to know when to break off an engagement. Sitting Bull increasingly demonstrated this kind of restraint as he reached his thirtieth year, and Lakota elders accordingly asked him to join the Silent Eaters. This society, of only about twenty men, had a special charge. Jumping Bull was a member, but the group excluded both of Sitting Bull's uncles because they were chiefs. The Silent Eaters met often late at night to eat in silence and then discuss crucial tribal matters. Its constitution included men from several different *wicotipis* and even a few men from other *tiospayes*. Accordingly, it set as its agenda discussions regarding the relationship of the various Hunkpapa *wicotipis* and how they interacted with other Lakota bands. According to White Bull, they addressed ways to "improve the mode of living of the [Lakota] tribe or to better the ways of getting out of trouble."

After war broke out with the Americans, the Silent Eaters became a highly important council of elders that discussed ways in which the Hunkpapa, Minneconjous, Sans Arcs, and even the factions of Oglalas, Brulés, and Yanktonais should deal with the invading Americans. It included the bravest warriors of the society, and it had the special charge to consider offers of peace. Indeed, the Silent Eaters seemed to have some major say over whether the society should remain at war or sue for peace. It had considerable influence with the society of hereditary chiefs who sat in the middle of camp and discussed daily matters. Some of the elders who sat with the hereditary chiefs also joined the Silent Eaters. It was the one society that had influence with both the hereditary chiefs and the male societies.

But even though Sitting Bull possessed a plethora of positions and honors, the status acquired from them did not give him the powers necessary to effectively confront the natural factionalism inherent in Lakota tribal politics. The constant movement to acquire game and the attending breakdown into small lodge groups for much of the year meant that both male societies and chief's societies did not meet for long periods. Nevertheless, the pressures grew more intense with each passing year as American armies and settler wagon trains increased their invasions of Lakota lands after 1864. To some degree, then, this constant harassment prompted continued reevaluation by various Lakota and Hunkpapa political leaders as they searched for ways to resist the aggression.

With Sitting Bull's rise to power in the Strong Hearts, his role as a Silent Eater, and his success in war, it was inevitable that he would be asked to join the Fox Society. Although the date seems quite late, White Bull indicated that the invitation arrived about 1860. His membership in this group gave him access to other chapters in other bands. Indeed, a Fox Society member often possessed membership in two different bands, White Bull being a member of both the Minneconjou and Sans Arc Fox Societies. What made membership in the Fox Society so important was that when the various *tiospayes* of the Lakota people came together each spring, the tribal council generally selected it to serve as the soldiers' lodge, or the *akicita*. This seemed appropriate since the large encampments often attracted people from several different Hunkpapa *tiospayes*, as well as other Lakota bands, such as the Oglalas and Brulés, and even other tribes, such as the Yanktonais, Yanktons, and Sissetons.

Though the Fox Society would have been important to the evolution of the Hunkpapa band under normal circumstances, its power and influence grew as Americans became more belligerent in dealing with the northern Sioux. And Fox Society members used their prestige to preach unity, noting the growing differences between the agency Indians and those who remained on the plains in the hunting camps. They also increasingly condemned the Americans for their aggressiveness.

Despite these efforts, Bear's Rib (the younger) decided in 1864 that it was better for his small *wicotipi* to stay permanently near the Missouri River agencies where they received food allotments. A few years later, Running Antelope followed him. Two of the seven Hunkpapa *wicotipis* had decided against resisting the advance of the Americans. This created very bad feelings between the groups that still remained hunters and warriors and those that the Americans called the agency "loafers."

Just as Lakota society seemed on the verge of polarization—probably in 1867—the Fox Society of the Hunkpapa band made Sitting Bull a *blotaunka*. The appointment lasted only as long as a good many Fox warriors respected it, but it did entail the right to lead war parties, select scouts, and maintain some control of the various soldiers' lodges that were necessary when many different villages came together. But there were other *blotaunkas* within the same society, including two men who clearly competed with Sitting Bull—No Neck and Gall. Both younger men than Sitting Bull, they too had the same rights, creating conflicting spheres of influence. Nevertheless, as a key war leader of the largest, most significant male society in the northern Lakota camps, Sitting Bull would have much to say about the involvement of his people with the Americans.

Considerable evidence suggests that Sitting Bull did have his way, becoming an outspoken opponent of any negotiation with the Americans and a strong critic of the agency Indians. And opposition to the agency Indians sharpened the Lakota sense of nationhood by better defining and contrasting esteemed cultural values. But Sitting Bull's growing dislike of the Americans and the agency loafers seemed matched at times by the animosity that No Neck and Gall had for him. Frank Grouard, who lived with Sitting Bull's people in the early 1870s, found that Gall and No Neck opposed his every effort. These two war leaders clearly advocated treating with the United States in the late 1860s, even when they seemed to have little idea what this involved. Gall and No Neck even opposed Sitting Bull when he convinced the Chiefs' Society to honor his adoption of the young American, Grouard. Sitting Bull had to assign several of his soldiers to protect Grouard twenty-four hours a day in order to prevent the No Neck–Gall faction from killing him.

Given this competition, which had apparently increased in the latter 1860s, Black Moon and Four Horns decided to make one last effort to secure a higher degree of authority for Sitting Bull. This effort seemed necessary given the factionalism within the society and the growing threat that it faced from the Americans. Sometime, very likely in the spring of 1868, Four Horns had Sitting Bull anointed as a *wakiconza,* a position commonly found among the Oglala and Brulé but never before used among the Hunkpapa. This position entailed arbitrating disputes when they arose, selecting the various *akicita* from the many different bands, and helping make decisions regarding war or peace, a judgment usually left up to the Chiefs' Society and the Silent Eaters. *Wakiconzas,* as one observer put it, were "half warrior, half peace maker." Most important, *wakiconzas* had the capacity of advising a village gathering consisting of many different bands and tribal factions.

Many years later, One Bull suggested that this ceremony resulted in Sitting Bull being made "the Supreme Chief of the Sioux Nation." Oral history accounts of the ceremony that anointed Sitting Bull do suggest that his elevation to a *wakiconza* was a magnificent affair, attended by four of the Hunkpapa hair-coat wearers as well as the leading chiefs of the Minneconjous and Sans Arc. Crazy Horse, an Oglala *blotaunka* of the Fox Society, was also in attendance and apparently gave his approval. During the ceremony, bearers carried Sitting Bull into a large circle on a buffalo robe and "crowned" him with a magnificent headdress.

But One Bull exaggerated. *Wakiconzas* never had such exalted power. Red Cloud had tried to assume such a position among the Oglalas, hoping to incorporate all the northern bands under his influence, and he had failed. *Wakiconzas,* then, were generally elders who had gained reputations for thoughtfulness and oratory. They did no fighting but directed large war parties. In large multiband Oglala camps, there generally were four of them who worked as an "executive," making sure that the camp functioned smoothly. Such men did have immediate access to the Chiefs' Society, and they spoke in council. They even possessed the ability to call a council of chiefs and elders and to speak directly to it. What Four Horns had tried to do, then, was to take the most respected war chief of his *wicotipi*, a man who had become a leader in several major male societies, and entrust him with civil authority. One Bull even suggests that Four Horns and the other hair-coat wearers stepped aside in order to give Sitting Bull a free reign, a claim that cannot be substantiated.

Despite testimony from the 1930s, taken from Sitting Bull's nephew, this new position was temporary, dependent on the willingness of people from several different bands and tribes to listen and accept the advice of the man who held it. No Neck and Gall, jealous competitors, also had gained reputations as *blotaunkas*, and they would listen and follow Sitting Bull only when it suited them. They had attended the ceremony in which Sitting Bull was elevated to his new post, but such a courtesy was common. The leaders of the *wicotipi* that Sitting Bull belonged to had every right to put their relative forward for the most exulted position.

But hair-coat wearers, such as Four Horns and Black Moon, did not command *blotaunkas* of another *wicotipi*. More important, No Neck and Gall received their badges of authority from male societies, much as Sitting Bull. Gall and No Neck viewed this ceremony as exactly what it was—an obvious attempt to elevate a relative and convince people to follow him.

Nevertheless, this man Sitting Bull had every intention of using his new position to end the factionalism and polarization that had been growing among his people and to forge a powerful and united Sioux nation to meet the American threat. Certainly, Sitting Bull had arrived at a station in life where he had achieved all the marks of status and accomplishment that his society could bestow on him. But it was status and rank in a nation that lacked permanent political structure and definition. Even Sitting Bull knew that Lakota leaders did not rule—

they led through persuasion, oratory, and example. But would the people listen?

As trouble with the Americans escalated, then, Sitting Bull sought to have his people coalesce around him. He hoped they would do so not because of his exalted position as supreme chief, but because of the very same reasons that his uncles and other relatives had pushed him into the limelight—Sitting Bull possessed the charisma, the training, and the ability to defend his land and his nation.

Finally, Sitting Bull had the power to draw from an inner strength that his competitors lacked. He had a unique relationship with *Wakantanka.* His people would listen to him for the simple reason that he, more so than Gall, No Neck, or even Crazy Horse, possessed that special understanding of the nature of things to come that would be crucial in preserving the Lakota nation and its way of life.

Even the Americans came to appreciate this in the early 1870s. Their reports and letters increasingly spoke of "Sitting Bull's hostiles," and of his influence. If not in fact an omnipotent leader, Sitting Bull wielded influence that threatened the continued expansion of the United States, and, unlike Red Cloud, he would not negotiate.

CHAPTER 3

Sitting Bull and the Defense of the Lakota Homeland

❖
❖

There is no question that Sitting Bull enjoyed his new role as *wakiconza* of the Hunkpapa people since it offered him more of an opportunity to speak up in council. *Blotaunkas* generally lacked the status to speak, and most of the time, they listened. But though Sitting Bull gained status through his new position, he lacked a thorough understanding of how to proceed. The Americans did have much to offer in terms of goods. Even Sitting Bull had found the new repeating rifles marvelous hunting tools, and he had virtually discarded his bows and arrows for firearms. More important, word arrived over the spring of 1868 that Americans wished to speak with him and his fellow chiefs. They said they wanted peace.

That spring, the Lakota camps that came together for the sun dance on the Powder River heard nothing but talk of peace. Even Sitting Bull's jealous competitors, Gall and No Neck, wondered what it meant. These younger men had become fine hunters and warriors. Their relatives also had been successful in elevating them to positions as *blotaunkas*. But their families lacked hereditary leaders such as Four Horns and Black Moon, and they had to sit by as the Chiefs' Society invited Sitting Bull into the their chambers and talked of this new idea, peace with the Americans. After listening to the chiefs speak their mind, Sitting Bull then also ate with the Silent Eaters, listening to all views.

This notion of peace seemed quite contradictory to many. It had been General Sully who had attacked the Lakota in 1864 for no reason. Everyone remembered this. Sitting Bull had also spent much time talking with the eastern Dakota Indians who had been forced to flee Minnesota in 1862. One of their leaders, Inkpaduta, was a friend and had nothing good to say about Americans. Finally, Sitting Bull and other chiefs had listened to the Cheyennes and Arapahos who occasionally visited them. They spoke often of the dreadful 1864 massacre of their people at Sand Creek in southeastern Colorado. American soldiers had literally cut up their people, doing horrible things to women and children. Sitting Bull wondered how such people could now speak of peace. It had been only four years since Sully's invasion and the attack at Sand Creek. Even as the talk went on, Sitting Bull helped form raiding parties that attacked the hated American garrisons on the Missouri, killing herders, wood choppers, and mailmen near Fort Buford.

But as the parties returned in the spring of 1868, and festivities got underway, good news arrived. The American peace delegation sent west would include the trusted friend of the Indian, the Catholic Jesuit Pierre-Jean De Smet, as well as many of the relatives of the Hunkpapas now attached to the reservation. Everyone, Indian or not, knew De Smet, who had gone to the Rockies three decades before. He traveled freely on the plains, armed only with a Bible. De Smet's assistance had been requested by the Bureau of Indian Affairs, which felt it necessary to acquire the signatures of Hunkpapa leaders on the Treaty of 1868 for the agreement to have any meaning. With Red Cloud seemingly willing to sign and settle on a reservation, the only obstacle seemed to be the northern bands.

De Smet arrived at Fort Rice on the Missouri with great fanfare on May 24 and promptly sent tobacco as a present to the Hunkpapas and associated *tiospayes* out on the Powder River. Sitting Bull immediately responded, sending a message to De Smet: I will "shake you by the hand," the chief promised and "hear your word." But the newly appointed *wakiconza* indicated that he would do this from the position of strength. "I am well formed by nature," he said, "half soldier [*blotaunka*] and half chief [*wakiconza*]." He would listen, but he still distrusted the Americans, and though he looked forward to seeing the "loafer" element from the reservations, he also questioned their loyalty.

This pleasant exchange made many of the "loafers" from the camp near Fort Rice less apprehensive about accompanying De Smet. Indeed, the priest put together a large party that included the Indian trader Charles Galpin, his Hunkpapa wife, Matilda, and a whole host of Hunkpapa men. The list included such dignitaries as Running Antelope, still a hair-coat wearer, young Bear's Rib, whose father had been gunned down by Hunkpapas for accepting annuities in 1862, and Two Bears, a minor chief of the accommodation element. Several dozen other men came along to watch.

This entourage reached the upper Yellowstone River in late June, where an advance of Hunkpapa scouts sent out by Sitting Bull met them. Proceeding, De Smet suddenly descended into the Powder River valley, where lodges dotted the bottomland. The main camp alone housed nearly five thousand Lakota. Hoards of them came forward almost overwhelming the priest in their efforts to see and touch the Blackrobe. Suddenly Sitting Bull appeared, splendidly dressed, and according to Galpin, who kept a journal, ordered his Fox *akicita* to disperse the people. "He then told the braves to take charge of us," Galpin noted, "to see that we had plenty to eat and drink, and not under any circumstances to allow either of us [Galpin or De Smet] to go far." Obviously, Sitting Bull feared that some of his own men might try to sabotage the peace talks that were about to begin. He ordered that the luggage of both men be put in his tent, where the delegates would sleep. Four Horns and Black Moon moved in as well.

The council opened on June 20 inside a huge council house formed from nearly two dozen tepees. De Smet estimated that five hundred Lakota men settled into the soft buffalo robes that covered the bare earth. Four Horns acted as master of ceremonies, opening the session with the peace pipe to ensure that everyone spoke the truth, for the words would ascend to *Wakantanka* who knew the truth. Black Moon, another hair-coat wearer, took station next to Four Horns; they obviously were the most senior men in the council. Behind them sat the *blotaunkas*. De Smet later pointed out that the war chiefs and their soldiers sat "according to the rank" that they held in their societies and *tiospayes*. As the affair got underway, men rose to speak based on the same system of rank.

As customary, after the pipe had been passed, Black Moon rose to ask that De Smet present his message. The Jesuit did so with gusto, asking that the Lakota end the bloodshed of the past few years and embrace peace. He offered as a present the banner that he carried into camp, elaborating that its symbol, a depiction of the Virgin Mary, stood for peace. Black Moon responded, being careful not to insult the obvious good intentions of the priest. He did have a litany of abuses that he wished to discuss, however, and little would dissuade him from his object. "We have been forced to hate the whites," he said, "let them treat us like brothers and the war will cease." The forts and the soldiers on the Missouri River clearly were the sticking point, as Black Moon argued that they took too much timber and scared away the game. The overland wagon trains did the same. And the soldiers, well, Black Moon could not understand how they could kill women and children as they had done at Sand Creek.

Sitting Bull next rose to address the Jesuit. He rambled a bit, obviously nervous in his first address of magnitude. He did finally concede that a peace council at Fort Rice—De Smet's ultimate objective—could be a good thing. But he wanted it perfectly understood that he had no intention of selling any land. Increasingly, the issue of land boundaries became a defining element in Lakota nationhood even though it really had never been one before. The Americans had helped make it so, pushing the Indians to define their territories so that purchases could be made. This had often caused confusion in Indian councils, and Sitting Bull categorically concluded in 1868 that his people no longer had any land to sell.

As his speech rambled on, Sitting Bull also demanded that the American soldiers abandon their forts. The chief would not attend any councils within the confines of a military post, and future peace, he felt, depended on the departure of the soldiers. Unfortunately, a delegation led by Gall had already formed to accompany De Smet east. Sitting Bull did not voice disappointment, but he obviously realized that they had been coaxed into doing this by the collaborationists that De Smet had brought with him. These men, Two Bears and Running Antelope, spoke next.

Two Bear's speech contrasted with Sitting Bull's. He found nothing to fear from either the forts or the wagon trains, and pointedly said that he was "troubled" by the hostile nature of his Hunkpapa relatives. For his part, he intended to accept De Smet's offer of peace. Running Antelope said much the same. "I have been listening to the good words of the whites for many years," he said matter of factly. Ever the diplomat, Running Antelope then put a new twist into the debate, noting that the Hunkpapas and the Americans were not responsible for the troubles of late, but rather the eastern Sioux were. He blamed Inkpaduta for the fighting in 1863–1864 and some of the raiding, and he too recommended peace.

On such a note, the first major council between the Hunkpapa and a representative of the United States came to an end. It had been informative and even friendly. On departure, De Smet honored Sitting Bull with a beautiful present—a large crucifix that the chief would constantly wear around his neck. Sitting Bull, Four Horns, and Black Moon would sign no treaties. But they would stop fighting if the Americans left them alone. Although the council did reveal to some extent the divisiveness among the Hunkpapa *wicotipis*, the senior leadership seemed to speak with one voice.

Yet Galpin and De Smet had convinced a large contingent of younger men under Gall to return with them to Fort Rice. In early July, along with many Yanktonais, Blackfoot, and Missouri River Lakotas—mostly "loafers"—Gall signed the 1868 treaty that ostensibly surrendered much of the prime hunting grounds of his people. Gall, thirty years old and a novice in politics, seemed to think that the treaty that he signed would result in the evacuation of the military posts and the expulsion from the upper Missouri of all Americans. There is not much evidence that even collaborators such as Running Antelope and Two Bears understood that the treaty would surrender all lands north of Fort Rice and eventually give up hunting grounds west of the Black Hills when the game gave out. For certain, even the American negotiators could not have been deceived into believing that this piece of paper would bring peace to the plains.

But astonishingly, the treaty did seem to lessen the fighting. By 1869, Sitting Bull had moved his people permanently into the Yellowstone River valley and its major tributaries, the Powder and Big Horn Rivers. The shift had occurred primarily because the lands adjacent to the central Missouri no longer contained buffalo, the remaining herds now being all west of the Bad Lands. Lakota hunters even ranged as far north as the Milk River in northern Montana and the Musselshell River in central Montana during times of scarcity. Even though a few small raiding parties, probably led by the minor war chiefs from the male societies, returned to attack Forts Buford and Rice thereafter, the threat in the east diminished appreciably. Sitting Bull took no part in any of these minor conflicts, remaining in the west.

The autumn of peace also sprung from the growing machinations over the legal right of way for the rapidly expanding Northern Pacific Railroad. The road hoped to connect Duluth, Minnesota, on Lake Superior with the Pacific Ocean, and its planners recognized that the shortest route west went through the Yellowstone River valley, the new home of the hunting

Sioux. Although little debate existed over whether the government had the right to enter this region—the treaty of 1868 had granted to railroads right of ways—Commissioner of Indian Affairs Francis A. Walker concluded that the Sioux could be convinced to accept the road peacefully if they were fed.

With a substantial appropriation from Congress, Walker ordered the construction of a new agency, called Fort Peck, near the confluence of the Milk River and the Missouri. In the spring of 1871, Walker's policy seemed to be working as several thousand Yanktonais, Sissetons, and Wahpetons (the latter two tribes being refugees from Minnesota) came to settle near the new agency, scaring off the local Assiniboins and Gros Ventres who had inhabited the region. It did not take long for the Hunkpapa to find this new establishment, some smaller *wicotipis* appearing at Fort Peck within a few days of the arrival of their Yanktonai kinsmen. Indeed, in September, Sitting Bull and a small party approached the fort stockade and proposed to trade. Throughout the fall, others from his lodge group appeared, and by winter, Black Moon had met with the agent and indicated a willingness to remain at peace.

Buttressed by such good fortune, Congress appropriated more money and stocked the Fort Peck warehouses. For his part, Commissioner Walker helped select another delegation to treat with the northern bands of hunting Sioux. Under the charge of Assistant Secretary of the Interior Benjamin R. Cowen, the commission spent the spring of 1872 planning the event, contacting officials at Fort Rice so that a large delegation of agency Hunkpapas from the Missouri might be present. The agency Indians who agreed to go, included Running Antelope, Two Bears, Bear's Rib (the younger), and at least a dozen others. Among the lesser dignitaries was young Charging Bear, better known in later years as John Grass.

To round out this imposing collection of dignitaries, the government invited agent J. W. Daniels to bring up a few Oglala Sioux leaders from his agency near the Platte River. Red Cloud refused, but a few minor leaders, including Red Dog agreed to the agent's request. Red Dog was an affable man with decidedly pro-American tendencies. Daniels, on the other hand, was the protege of the Episcopalian Bishop Henry Whipple, a strong advocate of the peace policy. But Daniels had other value. He had worked for two decades among the eastern, or Dakota, Sioux in Minnesota, and he spoke the Dakota language with some proficiency. His report revealed much about conditions in the Yellowstone country.

Commissioner Cowen found it more difficult to bring his council together than he had originally expected. Sitting Bull simply failed to show up. And both Cowen and Daniels learned very quickly that without his consent, nothing could be done. Sitting Bull and Black Moon, they concluded, had "great influence among the Teton." But this came as a surprise to both Cowen and Daniels, who had been told by Red Cloud and Spotted Tail that Sitting Bull was nothing more than "a mean-spirited sort of fellow with but little or no influence." Obviously, the failure of the collaborationists, Red Cloud and Spotted Tail, to have any influence over the hunting bands had sorely hurt their pride.

Probing deeper into the power structure of the hunting bands, the commission concluded that peace would have to be negotiated with Sitting Bull for it to have any meaning. Warriors of some note and even chiefs removed their coup feathers from their head when they sat in Sitting Bull's presence. More important, Sitting Bull now so completely despised the agency collaborationists—perhaps a result of his experience with them during the De Smet council—that he refused to sit with them in council. The few Hunkpapas who did talk with the commissioners also indicated that they felt that the agency Indians had come west only to acquire a portion of the presents. Cowen sent Running Antelope and the others home to avoid trouble, but he acted too late to appease Sitting Bull and the hunting bands.

Finally, on August 21, 1872, the commissioners sat down with a collection of Hunkpapas, Minneconjous, and Sans Arcs. Sitting Bull had sent his brother-in-law, His-Horse-Looking, to listen. Makes Room represented the Minneconjous. But Black

Moon, No Neck, Four Horns, and Sitting Bull—the very leadership of the northern bands—were all absent. That the government had not abandoned any of the Missouri River forts after the 1868 treaty had been noted by every Hunkpapa chief. Even more perplexing, even as they spoke, the hunter groups had become entangled with two invading American armies that were then protecting surveying parties along the Yellowstone River, producing several skirmishes.

Nevertheless, commissioner Cowen tried to coax an agreement out of the few representatives who were present. He wondered if the Indians might agree to accept the railroad, which was laying track between Fargo and Bismarck, North Dakota. In addition, he hoped that the leaders of the northern bands would consent to go to Washington to work out the details. His-Horse-Looking listened patiently and said only this: Sitting Bull had said, "Tell the white men if they will find [an] honest one, he [Sitting Bull] will talk with him." Cowen mused afterward in his correspondence about what exactly that meant. His-Horse-Looking never revealed whether or not he found such a man among the commissioners.

Through the various Indians at Fort Peck, agent Daniels did arrive at a fair estimate of the strength of the northern bands and the attitudes of the various chiefs. Although he seemed convinced that Sitting Bull had immeasurable prestige as a war leader, No Neck also possessed a large following among the Hunkpapas. Sitting Bull, Black Moon, and Four Horns actually lorded over a smaller *wicotipi* than No Neck. When combined, these chiefs headed at least 450 lodges, or 600 to 800 men. This figure likely included some Sans Arcs and Minneconjous, but not the Sissetons, Wahpetons, and Yanktonais, who possessed another 260 lodges. These latter three tribes listened to Sitting Bull and the other northern chiefs but acted mostly in their own self-interests.

Daniels had also brought with him three representatives from the Oglalas whom he sent eastward into the Hunkpapa camps as soon as they reached Fort Peck. Their leader, Red Dog, had become a strong supporter of the reservation system and carried with him an address from Red Cloud. Reaching the Hunkpapas and their allies in camp at the mouth of the Powder River, Red Dog spoke strongly about what the government had done for the Indians in the south. The camp seemed to be divided over the speech, the chiefs generally receiving it positively. Red Dog later told Daniels that most of the chiefs, including presumably Sitting Bull, seemed unsure of what to say about the Northern Pacific Railroad. But then it remained unclear at this time what direction the road would eventually take, only a few officials such as Daniels being fully informed.

Red Dog had also discovered that many of the northern Indians had a very negative view of the United States. Even more disturbing, Daniels thought, were the large numbers of young Oglalas and Brulé Lakotas, as well as Cheyennes and Arapahoes, who regularly abandoned their agency to commune with the Yellowstone River Sioux. Though he tried to keep them near his agency by giving them only fifteen days rations at a time, this seldom worked, and they could easily add another thousand men to the hunting groups. In addition, the reservation Indians often had access to firearms and munitions that the hunting bands lacked. Many young firebrands from the reservations seemed discontent with their situation and with their chiefs, and small segments of them spent more and more time with the hunting groups, especially during the summer when the buffalo could be found and life on the plains was good.

While the events at Fort Peck unfolded, the conflict that Cowen and Daniels had been so confident that they could forestall started afresh. The problem developed along the Yellowstone River not far from the main camp of Sitting Bull's followers. That August, as Cowen called out to the Sioux, two heavily guarded parties of railroad surveyors proceeded into the Yellowstone Valley, the heartland of the Lakota hunting bands. One command, under Colonel David S. Stanley, left from Fort Rice, and another, stationed in Montana, departed from Bozeman, under the leadership of Major Eugene M. Baker.

Some intimation of the trouble that this would bring had occurred the previous April when a young Sans Arc named Spotted Eagle had visited Stanley along the Missouri River. He had told the colonel that the Lakotas would never agree to have the railroad run through the Yellowstone River valley. "He would fight the railroad people as long as he lived," Spotted Eagle gruffly said to Stanley. The news of these parties had reached the Lakota camps under Sitting Bull and the other Hunkpapa leaders by summer and, in early August, as they heard pleas from Cowen to visit Fort Peck, they saw soldiers invading their lands from two directions.

The chiefs with Sitting Bull initially wished to avoid conflict. Along these lines, the Chiefs' Society ordered the war chiefs to use the *akicita* to prevent the young men from attacking the American parties. This allowed the two military parties to make considerable progress into the valley. But finally the chiefs could not hold the young men, and a party of Brulés— the very young men whom Daniels had hoped to keep out of hunter camps—evaded the Lakota soldiers and struck Major Baker's command on August 13. Soon other Hunkpapa and Sans Arc young men joined them, White Bull himself disobeying the orders of the *akicita* and surging ahead to get at the American soldiers. Soon Baker's command of nearly five hundred fell under a heavy fire that raged into the night.

The "battle" at Arrow Creek, named for a small tributary of the Yellowstone, continued into the next day. As the sun came up, the soldiers had established a defensive line in the thickets of the river bank, but the Lakota warriors completely encircled them. Young Lakota men on horseback rode up and down the wide valley, clinging to the manes of their horses and firing at the troops. Such sport proved ineffective, however, since Baker's infantry had dug into the bank of the river. It gave the Lakota young men an opportunity to prove their valor, but it provided no coups. A rash young man named Plenty Lice made the only attempt to ride into the very lines of the soldiers, but the infantry promptly killed him. His friends failed to retrieve his body, and the American troops built a bonfire and threw his corpse into it.

As the morning came, Sitting Bull and Crazy Horse came down to the river to observe the events. As the party with the war chiefs looked down on the reckless young men from a high hill, dashing back and forth in front of the troops, suddenly they saw Sitting Bull walk down the hill into the river valley below. They asked him where he was going, and he simply replied, whoever "wishes to smoke with me, come." White Bull, two Cheyennes, and a Hunkpapa accepted the invitation. Moving closer and closer to the soldiers, finally Sitting Bull came within range of the rifles and, with little display, sat down in the sand and pulled out his pipe.

Undisturbed by the raucousness going on all around him, Sitting Bull carefully removed his flint and steel from his pipe pouch, loaded his catlinite pipe, and lit the tobacco. He drew a long drag and passed it to his friends, who, in the meantime, noticed that the American soldiers were now concentrating their fire on the small group of men sitting in the sand. Bullets whizzed above their heads and hit beside them. But Sitting Bull sat undisturbed, handing his pipe to the others in a deliberate fashion. Even the young horsemen who had been challenging the soldiers took notice of the event, one of them riding over to where the smokers sat. As he arrived, a bullet smashed into his body, and he fell dead in front of the small group. White Bull later confessed that he had never before smoked a pipe so rapidly. But Sitting Bull took his time, stopping to gaze at the entrenched troops as he cleaned the bowl with a stick and slowly walked back up the bluff.

The observers on the hill, including Crazy Horse, could see that such an act of bravery had no precedent even among the bravest of warriors. Crazy Horse, increasingly a friend of Sitting Bull's but also his competitor, could not stand to sit and do nothing. As the smoking party retreated, he mounted his horse and took one last run along the lines of the Americans. A bullet pierced the animal's breast and brought Crazy Horse crashing to the ground. He quickly ran from the battlefield, thus, ending the skirmish known as the battle of Arrow Creek.

Sitting Bull and his fellow tribesmen then withdraw to check on yet another skirmish that had broken out between other Hunkpapas led by young Gall and Colonel Stanley's command farther down the Yellowstone. Gall had watched Stanley as he slowly moved his infantry troops up the Missouri and into the Yellowstone. On one occasion, he tried to surprise a surveyor who strayed too far from the party. But Stanley's troops arrived just in time to save him. On another, Gall tried to open a conversation with Stanley, asking what he was doing in Sioux country. Both sides were too edgy to talk, however, and soon the shooting broke out again.

On August 21, Sitting Bull arrived. The very day in which commissioner Cowen sat down with the remnant of Sioux at Fort Peck, the Hunkpapa chief that he hoped to see, turned to directing the battle against Stanley. Young warriors went this way and that, attempting to drive off mule and horse herds on some occasions and trying to lure the infantrymen out into the open on others. Though the fighting never produced many casualties, the constant sniping completely broke the concentration of the engineers and brought Stanley to the point of retreat. The colonel failed to link up with Baker, and he turned eastward in disgust, leaving much of the proposed roadbed along the Yellowstone undetermined.

The army in Washington read the reports of both Baker and Stanley with considerable interest. No less a person than General William Tecumseh Sherman saw the affair as an outrage. The Americans had a right to be in the Yellowstone valley, he said, and the Northern Pacific Railroad was "a national enterprise" that had to be protected. Considerable progress already had been made on the road, the first trains reaching Bismarck during the summer of 1873. Given such a means of transportation, it became much cheaper to support military efforts in the region, using the rails to bring in food and grain for horses.

General Sherman realized that the sorts of garrisons generally stationed along the Missouri River—almost entirely infantry—would never bring the Sioux to submission. Indeed, they often suffered insult at the hands of a handful of mounted Indians. But with the rails in place, it became possible to order the Seventh Cavalry to the upper Missouri, troops that offered an important offensive capability. More important, the seven-hundred-strong Seventh Cavalry was commanded by Lieutenant Colonel George Armstrong Custer. Custer had had a brilliant career in the Civil War, showing bravery and determination at every chance. Sherman ordered Custer and his unit to the new fort called Abraham Lincoln, built just outside Bismarck, confident that the Seventh would attack rather than dig foxholes.

Custer wasted little time in searching out his Lakota adversaries. He launched a combined cavalry–infantry expedition into the Yellowstone River valley in the summer of 1873. Though the expedition was once again meant to continue the surveying, Custer had a reputation of taking war to the Indians. He had gained fame for overrunning a Cheyenne and Arapahoe village during the winter of 1868 on the Washita River in western Oklahoma. He later claimed that his troops had killed only a dozen or so women and children in the attack, but the Indians knew the figure was much higher. Custer liked to surprise Indians when they were most vulnerable—while feeling secure in their villages.

Custer clearly had such designs regarding Sitting Bull's people. His troop reached the mouth of the Tongue River by early August. Sitting Bull and about four hundred lodges of Hunkpapas lay directly in his path. As Custer approached, the Sioux laid a trap, using decoys in an attempt to isolate two companies of cavalry led by Custer himself. But the ruse failed when Custer took cover in some timber and called on Stanley's infantry to come to his support. With a much larger force, Custer then pushed ahead hoping to find the elusive village of Sitting Bull. Very wisely, Sitting Bull moved his people over to the other bank of the Yellowstone and used small parties to harass the American cavalry. Then Custer broke off, moving north into the Musselshell River valley and out of the range of the Lakota.

The army had learned valuable lessens from the campaigns in 1872 and 1873. They had found the Indians without much trouble and had studied the countryside, coming to know the various tributaries of the Yellowstone River with considerable certainty. They also seemed confident after the skirmishes that Sitting Bull's young men would not stand and fight. Whenever a large force had been sent directly against the Indians, the latter had retreated. Forces of several hundred men, they concluded, were perfectly safe in the Yellowstone valley as long as they had plenty of ammunition and watched for ambushes.

But this confidence in strategy would have to wait further testing, for in 1873 a terrible financial panic hit Wall Street, and the Northern Pacific Railroad suddenly went broke. Engineers and surveyors departed for the east, leaving their newly made maps of the Yellowstone to gather dust. Newspaper editors in Bismarck, a frontier town that already styled itself as the "Chicago of the West," watched as the economy went into a nosedive.

Unfortunately for the Sioux, such financial difficulty brought renewed interest in the possible wealth of the Black Hills. Indeed, Colonel Custer, no longer able to use railroad surveyors as an excuse to campaign against Indians, decided the next year that he would survey the Black Hills. The War Department concurred after the colonel made it clear that he could look for a possible site to build an army post, ostensibly to protect the southern reservations from the northern Indians.

Custer remained in the field throughout most of the summer of 1874, but even before he returned to Fort Lincoln, news had been carried east of "Gold in the Black Hills." Actually, the prospectors with him found only a few nuggets, but with the depression in full swing, the "discovery" led to a rush. Americans who had lost everything now saw only riches. That the hills belonged only to the Sioux and that the government had pledged to keep Americans out of them seemed to disappear into the headlines. Train after train of Americans jumped off from the surrounding depots along the Platte and Missouri Rivers. The army published broadsides reaffirming their will to prevent such an invasion, but it did virtually nothing to stop the invasion. By 1875, the southern extremities of the Black Hills had been overrun.

Although Sitting Bull's Lakotas now hunted far from the southern extremities of the Black Hills, they knew well what the invasion meant. It simply brought the *wasicun* much closer to their hunting lands. And the Black Hills did play a sacred role in Sioux religion. Young Sioux men commonly sought their first visions in the hills, climbing to the top of one of the highest peaks to pray. Most men did this alone, and they returned to camp with an overwhelming appreciation for the mystery that the darkened hills revealed. The Black Hills were simply *wakan,* or mystical. The Lakota would never willingly give them up. Nevertheless, the *wasicuns* had taken them, and they had no intention of evacuating them. Sitting Bull could plainly see that the Americans had no respect for anyone, killing women and children when fighting and breaking sacred promises.

Even the reservation Sioux opposed the American invasion of the Black Hills. Red Cloud was outraged and demanded to go to Washington and rectify the injustice. In the spring of 1875, he got his wish. Promptly, he sent messengers to the northern bands calling on their chiefs to come in and accompany him. He wanted their support, and he especially hoped to lure in Crazy Horse and Black Twin, the two most respected Oglala leaders living off the reservation. Neither came. Red Cloud found it necessary to make the trip with Spotted Tail and a few lesser chiefs.

Once in Washington, they found that President Grant had no intention of seeing them. Instead, Secretary of Interior Columbus Delano greeted the party. The secretary tried to put the troubles on the plains into perspective. Even though the treaty of 1868 had granted them the Black Hills forever, he said, the government could not keep the *wasicuns* out. It would solve many problems, the secretary concluded, if the Sioux would agree to move to Indian Territory, or Oklahoma.

Red Cloud, somewhat dumbfounded, pretended not to understand this outrageous suggestion. It was the courteous thing to do. Instead, he demanded actions for reservation problems, especially attacking the quality of the food disbursement. But as the talks degenerated into a debate over the quality and quantity of food, often without any sense of the real issues that separated the two groups, the Indians became disgusted and went home.

But the question of the Black Hills did not go away. After the delegates returned, they soon found that the government was sending yet another commission to purchase or lease the hills. Under the direction of Edward Allison, the commission hoped to attract representatives of all the Lakota groups and get an agreement. In order to bring in the hunting bands, the commission hired Frank Grouard, one-time occupant of Sitting Bull's lodge, to go to the Powder River country and coax the most recalcitrant bands into Red Cloud Agency. Grouard knew of Sitting Bull's animosity toward him and agreed to go only after being paid $500.

Grouard found the hunting bands near the confluence of the Powder and Yellowstone Rivers, camped in five separate circles or *tiospayes*. A strong Oglala contingent recognized Crazy Horse and Black Twin as their leaders, the former being a war chief and the latter, a shirt wearer. The Sans Arc recognized Spotted Eagle as chief, and the Minneconjou heeded advice from Makes Room and his son, White Bull. A separate circle of Northern Cheyenne had also joined the coalition under their leader, Ice. Finally, the Hunkpapas, the largest group, still fell under the sway of Sitting Bull, No Neck, Four Horns, Black Moon, and Gall. These men had divided opinions on what should be done. Sitting Bull, however, made his views known immediately in council. He did not trust or like Grouard anymore, and he had no intention of going to Red Cloud Agency and selling the Black Hills.

Not everyone agreed with him. Crazy Horse had developed a fondness for Grouard, who recommended that the chiefs go in and negotiate. Indeed, when Grouard feared for his life—Sitting Bull had threatened to kill him some years before—Crazy Horse announced to everyone that they would have to kill him too if they had designs on his friend. But Crazy Horse elected to support Sitting Bull on the issue of negotiation. He too distrusted reservation officials and government commissioners. Only about four hundred Lakotas from the hunting camps went in to Red Cloud, led mostly by the Oglala chief Little Big Man.

The Allison commission sat down with the reservation chiefs in September and offered to buy the Black Hills. They haggled over price and at times, threatened to stop distributing annuities. But the words from Sitting Bull, presented by the representatives of the hunting bands, made it extremely difficult to reach agreement. He had said simply, "I will not go to the reservation. I have no land to sell. There is plenty of game for us. We have enough ammunition." And finally, "We don't want any *wasicuns* here." When even Spotted Tail seemed reticent, the commissioners gave up on getting an agreement. When back in Washington, they recommended that the government simply take the land by force.

With this purpose in mind, President Ulysses S. Grant called a high-level meeting in November 1875. The army had as its representative General Sherman, and the Department of Interior, which headed up the Indian Bureau, sent Secretary Delano. Consensus existed within this small group, and the president ordered that the Bureau of Indian Affairs step aside and let the army solve the problem. Sherman recommended that the hunting bands be sent an ultimatum. They must all report to a reservation by January 31, 1876, or be declared "hostile" and punished. The commissioner of Indian Affairs directed the various agents on December 6, 1875, to "notify Sitting Bull's band and other wild and lawless bands of Sioux Indians," that they must comply.

Even the most earnest student of history would have to search far and wide to find a more blatant disregard for the rights of Indians. The hunting bands were on their own land as outlined by the treaty of 1868. Buffalo still existed, and they had never agreed to give up this land. Although the president would later justify the order by arguing that the hunting bands had caused trouble in the Montana settlements as well as with the Crow and other tribes of the eastern mountain watershed, historically, the federal government had never made war on one tribal society to halt an occasional raid against another. President Grant issued the order to provoke war with the Sioux and, thus, justify the taking of the Black Hills.

The hunting bands under Sitting Bull and the others knew nothing of the change in Washington policy. They had, however, begun preparing for war not long after the first serious attempts had been made to invade their lands. The flirtations with the Fort Peck Indian agent, begun in 1871, had as an ulterior motive the need to acquire access to trade. Many Indians had been successful at acquiring new firearms and, for the first time, cartridges for breech loading and repeating rifles. Sitting Bull preferred a Winchester Model '73, a weapon that White Bull had apparently given him.

Other outlets of trade had been developed with the Canadian Métis, who had often competed with the plains Sioux for buffalo, but now, found trading for skins almost more lucrative than hunting. Grouard had witnessed a trade fair in which Sitting Bull's people got arms for hides in 1873, the last year that he spent with the band. Thereafter, some Métis even came overland during the winter on horse-drawn sleighs, doing a lucrative trade. By 1876, the hunting bands had better arms than they had ever possessed before, probably one-fourth of them owning repeating rifles.

But the Sioux remained unprepared for the type of warfare that the army intended to initiate. Certainly there is no evidence that the Indians knew what the deadline of January 31 meant. In a practical sense, it would have been impossible for them to move five hundred miles in the dead of winter to reservations. And, in fact, the agents never made much of an effort to implement the commissioner's order to force the hunting bands to come into the agencies. General Sherman knew all this better than anyone. But he wanted a winter deadline in order to launch a winter campaign. Indeed, he ordered his troops to prepare to march before the deadline had even passed, hoping to catch the hunting bands seemingly secure in their winter villages where they would be forced to defend their women and children.

The first troops left on this campaign from Fort Fetterman under the command of General George Crook in February 1876. A veteran of some ability, Crook unfortunately chose Colonel Joseph J. Reynolds to lead the cavalry, which he sent ahead. Reynolds had been ordered to scour the Powder River country and attack any village. To help guide the mission, Crook had hired none other than Frank Grouard, Sitting Bull's one-time adopted brother and friend to Crazy Horse. Sitting Bull had trained Grouard well. The guide bragged that he could find the Sioux even in heavy snow and excruciatingly cold weather. Reynolds, on the other hand, totally distrusted Grouard.

Nevertheless, on a cold, blustery morning, March 17, Grouard found a village, nestled in the protective Powder River valley near the present Wyoming–Montana border. Reynolds cautiously attacked with an overwhelming force, driving the seven to eight hundred Indians into the −30° weather. Reynolds had found Two Moon's camp, consisting mostly of northern Cheyennes, Minneconjous, and a few Oglalas. The Indians—men, women, and children—fled to the bluffs and hills as the troops captured most of the village's horses and prepared to burn the lodges.

At this point, Reynolds lost his nerve. Though the Indians kept up a rear-guard defense, mostly to protect their women and children, Reynolds concluded that they, in league with Grouard, intended to ambush him. He ordered retreat. The underarmed and outnumbered Indians rallied, recaptured their animals, and forced Reynolds to turn tail. The cowardice cost Reynolds a court-martial, but the Sioux and Cheyenne lost their homes in the dead of winter. They trudged north to the willing aid of Crazy Horse and Sitting Bull, whose villages were just above them on the Powder.

By spring, everyone in the hunting bands now knew what the government meant. Some Indians had come into the reservations. They reported Sitting Bull and the other chiefs to be outraged by the Reynolds attack. If there had been divided opinion in the past, everyone now seemed to sense that the Lakota and their Cheyenne allies were at war with the United States. In the councils along the Powder and Big Horn Rivers, the war leaders, or *blotaunkas,* gained more influence. The *akic-itas* mobilized, sending out scouts in every direction. The hunting bands expected troops to come and knew that garrisons were preparing campaigns in the south under General Crook, in the east at Fort Abraham Lincoln, where Custer's cavalry waited for grass to appear, and even north of them, where a large contingent of infantry had been assigned to General Alfred Terry to block the Sioux from crossing the Yellowstone.

General Philip H. Sheridan took overall command of the disposition of troops from a new headquarters established in Chicago. After surveying the situation, he concluded to attack the Sioux from three directions, Crook coming up from the south, Terry making it impossible for the Indians to flee across the Yellowstone River, and Custer hitting the villages from the east, with his Seventh Cavalry. For tactical purposes, Custer was placed under the command of Terry. The dashing, young lieutenant colonel was supposed to coordinate his movements with those of Terry. The plan seemed foolproof, and Sheridan expected a quick victory. Unfortunately, it had been a difficult winter, and the Missouri thawed very slowly. Sheridan had hoped to campaign in March, but he soon realized that the troops would not be able to engage the enemy until June.

Little did Sheridan realize what a fatal flaw this delay caused. Come spring, rumors spread across the reservations along the Missouri. The difficult winter had made it nearly impossible to get annuities to Red Cloud, Spotted Tail, or Cheyenne River Agency, and the warehouses were mostly bare. Word from the hunting camps offered a marked contrast, or so it would seem. Runners coming in told of plentiful buffalo in the Powder and Big Horn valleys. Many reservation Indians made plans to join the hunting bands as soon as the grass proved nutritious enough to support their horses.

Some of the informants who returned to the reservations also spoke of Sitting Bull. He had become more determined than ever to resist the *wasicuns* in the aftermath of the Reynolds attack, and everyone knew that he possessed amazing spiritual power. He had mastered the sacred ceremonies, possessed a remarkable charm, and could determine the will of *Wakantanka* through his unusual ability to receive visions. While Custer waited for the spring grasses to support his horses, the ponies on the reservations, much farther to the south, strengthened rapidly. Small parties of young men began leaving the reservations in May, bent on going out to hunt, dance, and see what knowledge *Wakantanka* had given to Sitting Bull.

The sight of "loafers" coming in from the agencies, hungry and eager for news, must have heartened Sitting Bull at this crucial juncture in Lakota history. He had argued for years that agency life was wrong and led to the dissipation and destitution of the people. The appearance of these people at his village certainly vindicated his counsel. If only he could hold the Sioux nation together and offer a united front against the Americans, he must have thought, they would certainly recognize the strength of the Lakota and their more eastern relatives and let them live in peace. Whatever the outcome, the threat of invasion and destruction, so prevalent since 1872, had produced consensus among the leaders with Sitting Bull. They would fight rather than be herded into reservations.

Just how many agency Indians left for the Powder River in May will never be known. The hunting bands likely had been losing followers since Daniels had estimated their numbers at roughly 450 lodges in 1872. But at the very least, the many young men who joined them early that spring of 1876 pushed back the number of lodges to roughly five hundred, and there may have been more. Yet within this group, one could count a disproportionate number of young fighting men. The war chiefs could probably bring together a thousand men.

But seldom if ever had any force this large been organized by the Lakota people. Their divided political structure prevented it. In addition, many young man had come out to dance and court, not fight. They had heard that Sitting Bull had staged a spectacular sun dance the year before, dressed only in a breech cloth and a war bonnet. With black painted face, yellow tinted body, and a black disk on his chest, representing the sun, he had danced and had his arms cut fifty times each to honor the new unity that had come to the hunting bands. Watching were thousands of people from the Hunkpapas, Oglalas, Minneconjous, Sans Arcs, Blackfoot, and northern Cheyenne. With the situation much more tense, everyone expected Sitting Bull to hold an even more impressive gala.

None were disappointed. In early June, as the trees budded along the central Rosebud River and the grass rose from the ground to support a massive herd of horses, the hunting bands came together again to dance and see what word might come from *Wakantanka* regarding their future. Two days before the dance, Sitting Bull wrapped his pipe with sage and, with his hair loose, went into the hills near the river and prayed. He called on *Wakantanka* to provide food for the people so that they might remain strong, and he prayed for the deliverance of the now united nation. "If you do this for me," he concluded, "I will sun dance two days and two nights and will give you a whole buffalo."

With the preliminaries out of the way, the dance began. This time Sitting Bull decided only to dance, joining several dozen other men who fasted for a day or two before entering the arena. As the sun came up the next day and reached far across the sky, Sitting Bull suddenly looked faint. Everyone could see that he was about to fall, and they grabbed and held him up. Finally, after he drank, he told Black Moon that a voice had suddenly startled him, and as he looked up, just below the sun, "he saw white men [soldiers] on horse back descending to the earth upon the Indian village." Sitting Bull thought they looked like grasshoppers, "their heads down and hats falling off." The voice said, "These soldiers do not possess ears."

Black Moon raced through the village announcing the vi-sion that Sitting Bull had seen of the battle. The soldiers would come right into their village, and all would be killed. The only caution made clear in the vision was that the Lakota warriors should not touch the bodies of the American soldiers or take spoils from them, or famine would surely follow for the na-tion. As Sitting Bull rested from the ordeal—he had temporar-ily lost his eyesight from staring into the sun for so long—he heard that soldiers had already been seen to the south along the headwaters of the Rosebud.

While the Sioux danced, the army's joint campaign got un-derway. Terry had taken up positions along the north bank of the Yellowstone in May, and Custer had left Fort Lincoln, checking the various tributaries of the Yellowstone for Indians as he headed west. Occasionally, Custer joined Terry at the Yel-lowstone River to confer and exchange information. These units had contingents of Indian scouts, mostly Arikaras and Crows, who everyone believed would eventually find the hunter villages.

With the same degree of confidence, Crook advanced in the south. His force totaled thirteen hundred men, so large that it took considerable planning just to feed the troops. Despite this size, Crook had mustered in a huge contingent of scouts, consisting of 175 Crows and 86 Shoshones. With them at his side, he marched into the Rosebud valley, certain that his scouts and his troops could handle any Sioux war party. In-deed, he expected the campaign to be short and decisive.

That same day, Cheyenne scouts, or wolves, as they were called, watched Crook from a far-off height. They raced back to the large, unified village of northern Indians, which since the sun dance, had moved westward toward the divide sepa-rating the Rosebud from the river called Little Big Horn. Here, on the evening of June 16, debate erupted both within the Chief's Society and among the various *blotaunkas* over what to do. Several war chiefs, including Sitting Bull and Crazy Horse, preached caution and patience. Let the soldiers come to the Indians. Support for this policy came from other Lakota chiefs who felt that the soldiers would negotiate before fighting. But the younger war chiefs would not listen. After dark, nearly five hundred young men rode off with them, forcing Crazy Horse and others to follow. Sitting Bull stayed behind.[1]

Crook had risen early on June 17, his force marching for two hours before taking a break near a bend in the Rosebud. Though the soldiers laid around in a leisurely manner, the Shoshones and Crows seemed tense, and some rode up the river a ways to scout the area. Suddenly, a huge mounted force of Lakotas and Cheyennes hit the Crows, sending them scurrying. A ferocious battle ensued, and the Sioux and Cheyenne quickly carried it to the unprepared Americans. Coming in on the sides of their horse, firing under the necks of the animals, the Sioux and Cheyenne warriors rode right through some of the American lines, knocking soldiers down in the traditional fashion of counting coup. Frightened American officers and men nearly broke and ran. The only thing that seemed to prevent a disaster was the fact that many of the cavalry troops had unsaddled their horses and had to fight. The shouting of the warriors reached such extremes that the troopers could not hold their animals.

As the battle raged, the casualties mounted on both sides. Finally in the afternoon, the warriors and soldiers disengaged. About a dozen Indians had died, and many others were wounded. The American troops had taken over fifty casualties, however, including ten deaths. A young American officer, Anson Mills, who commanded one of the companies, later

---

[1]Some sources suggest that Sitting Bull went with the war parties and eventually fought at the Battle of the Rosebud. Most of the oral history suggests, however, that he did not, probably on account of his sore eyes.

said, "we were lucky not to have been entirely vanquished." Crook called it a victory since he held the ground at day's end, but Mills later confided that it was a "humiliating defeat." Crook's surgeons even said that if the general proceeded to attack the village, which was certainly ahead, they would not stay with the dozens of wounded men. Crook had been unnerved and neutralized. He ordered a retreat to his base camp.

Once back in camp, the Sioux and Cheyenne victory celebration was tainted to some degree by the large losses. Crazy Horse knew that they had sent Crook reeling. With but six or seven hundred men, they had defeated an army of thirteen hundred, well supported by Indian allies. Yet when the victorious party arrived at the consolidated village in the high country east of the Rosebud, the women were already taking down the tepees. The Chiefs' Society had decided to move farther west into a stream called by the Sioux the Greasy Grass, or better known to the Americans as the Little Big Horn. It had better grass for the horses, and considerable game. Such provisions were necessary since more people came in from the agencies, anxious to hear the news.

These young men left the agencies in the east for a variety of reasons. Some simply wished to hunt for the summer and return to secure rations at the agencies when the snow began to fly. Others came to see relatives and catch up on the local gossip. Still, a large portion came to hear what Sitting Bull expected would happen, most realizing that the army intended to campaign against the hunting Sioux that summer.

Even James McLaughlin, Indian agent at Standing Rock and a great detractor of Sitting Bull's, later professed that Sitting Bull acted like a giant magnet, luring the young men away from the agencies. "He [Sitting Bull] had a great reputation on account of his medicine," McLaughlin concluded, "and the people at the agencies had come to believe that his medicine was invincible." Many of these young men came into Sitting Bull's camp and offered him presents, and as McLaughlin pointed out, the chief "used these present to great advantage in maintaining his popularity with the chiefs."

Just how many newcomers arrived in early and mid-June is again conjecture, but as the village on the Little Big Horn took shape, it held nearly twice as many lodges as when the hunting bands had come together in May. By June 24, upward of one thousand lodges lay on the western bank of the river. They had been placed in an orderly fashion, the Cheyennes leading the movement and building the camp circle farthest north. Following were the Oglalas, Brulés, Sans Arcs, Minneconjous, and Blackfoot. Finally, the Hunkpapa formed the last *tiospaye*, with Sitting Bull ordering the *akicita* of the band to act as rear guard. As they camped along the Little Big Horn, then, in this order, the Hunkpapa were farthest south, closest to the small tributary later called Reno Creek that offered the most favorable avenue of approach into the valley from the east.

With such a powerful gathering—now perfectly capable of sending forth two thousand men—many of the chiefs and most of the warriors felt secure. They could not imagine an army large enough to attack them. Accordingly, they had been celebrating the victory on the Rosebud, dancing into the night and lounging much of the day, feasting on a herd of antelope that had been discovered nearby. Scouts kept a close lookout to the south and to the north, but less attention was given to the east, the ground over which the camp had moved just a few days before.

To what degree Sitting Bull adhered to this rather lax attitude is impossible to determine. He did realize, as did many others, that the vicious battle with Crook had not resembled the struggle that he had predicted. Accordingly, he often avoided the dancing and went into the hills to pray, usually at dusk. White Bull accompanied him on this mission on the evening of June 24, with Sitting Bull crossing the Little Big Horn to the east and climbing to the top of a moderately sized hill that would later hold an obelisk with Custer's name attached.

Here in the twilight, Sitting Bull once again spoke to *Wakantanka*. He first gave offerings, smoking the pipe so that the words he spoke would be received as the truth, spreading bits of tobacco on the ground and presenting a buffalo robe to the all-powerful *Wakantanka*. Then he prayed. "Great Spirit, pity me," he began. "Father, save the tribe, I beg you. Pity me, we wish to live. Guard us against all misfortune or calamities."

The next morning, June 25, Colonel Custer and his cavalry arrived at the heights separating the Rosebud and Little Big Horn Rivers. Climbing to the top of a nearby ridge, the colonel discovered the haze that marked the Sioux campfires on the Little Big Horn. The Indian scouts, who had remarkable eye-sight, could even see the mass of horses west of the village.

Even though the troops had traveled through much of the night, Custer ordered boots and saddles for his 750 men. He ordered a fast trot, descending Reno Creek, hopeful of catching the Indians before they vanished in front of his men. He had only to recall the expedition of 1873 along the Yellow-stone, when the Sioux used bull boats made of hides to cross the Yellowstone River and escape his forces. This time would be different. He seemed to think that he had the element of surprise.

Custer's only real concern seemed to be whether all the Indians were camped below him on the Little Big Horn. As a precaution, he ordered Captain Frederick W. Benteen with a large force to scout south. A few miles farther on, he made yet another crucial decision. He ordered Major Marcus Reno with two hundred men to proceed west, cross the Little Big Horn, and strike the village on its southern extremity. Custer, mean-while, proceeded north, looking for a way to reach the village from the heights above with his remaining 204 men.

At that moment, Custer no doubt thought that he had achieved ultimate success. The Sioux village had little inkling that he was coming. Women, picking berries in the late morning sun, gave the alarm. Most of the men were still in their lodges. Horses grazed on the slopes both east and west of the river. Women and children played in the water of the Little Big Horn, oblivious to any threat. Suddenly a fuselage of gun fire erupted, well south of Sitting Bull's circle of lodges. It was

Reno, his men with drawn carbines, charging down on Sitting Bull's *tiospaye*. The vision had come true, and the bullets from Reno's men ripped through the tops of the tepees. The surprise had been complete.

Pandemonium broke loose in the village. Babies cried. Children rushed around madly looking for their mothers. One Cheyenne woman, Kate Bighead, later said that as she came rushing back into camp, one Sioux woman "just stayed in one spot, jumping up and down and screaming because she could not find her little son." Other women almost methodically turned to tearing down the tepees as fast as possible in order to flee. But the war chiefs and the leaders of the various soldiers' lodges sprung to action amid the chaos. Old men found weapons for the young and quickly painted the faces of the warriors. Young men started singing their war songs. "Were I to run away from the enemy, no one will consider me a man," the Fox Society song went. And more and more armed men from the central part of the village came to aid the Hunkpapas as Reno's men bore down on the tepees.

Sitting Bull reacted much like the other elders. He was now almost fifty years old, lame, and still probably somewhat blinded from the ordeal of the sun dance. But he did what he could, encouraging the men to defend the people. "Get busy and do something," he screamed, and then in a more encouraging voice, "brave up boys, it will be a hard time—brave up." Unable to fight, both Sitting Bull and Makes Room found horses for the women, Sitting Bull evacuating his mother and sister. He sent them off to the northwest to escape the firing. Then dressed in a buckskin shirt with hair fringe and displaying one feather in his head, he mounted a black horse and rode down to observe the battle.

Having helped organize the village's defense, Sitting Bull arrived late at the scene of what had been a horrendous struggle just south of his camp circle. A horde of young Sioux warriors had heroically met Reno head-on, forcing his retreat. His troop had difficulty crossing the Little Big Horn, forcing some soldiers to dismount. Once on the plain below the village, they soon discovered that the number of Indians increased rapidly and casualties mounted. A scout riding next to Reno took a bullet in the brain, and matter splattered over the major, unnerving him. As he turned, so did his troop who quickly lost heart. Had Reno reached Sitting Bull's tepees, forcing the Sioux and Cheyennes to look to their women and children, the entire outcome of the battle might have been different. But Sitting Bull appeared just as the last remnants of Reno's force recrossed the river, searching for a height from which to make a stand. Reno had lost over forty men in a short time, nearly one-fourth of his command.

Sitting Bull, after seeing that the soldiers were beaten and retreating, sought out his adopted nephew Old Bull. It had been Old Bull and Gall who had led the charge that had turned Reno back. Seeing a few straggling soldiers scurrying for cover, he told his relative to let them go. In Sitting Bull's vision, the chief had been told that he, personally, should not fight the soldiers who would fall into camp. He wished to respect that omen. The chief even temporarily saved the life of a soldier who was lying mortally wounded. The soldier asked for water, and Sitting Bull let him drink from a buffalo horn before he died.

Then Old Bull suggested that he lead the Hunkpapas still nearby against yet another contingent of soldiers that had been reported farther north on the east side of the river. Sitting Bull, who was better informed, told him no. The women and children needed protection, he said, and there were plenty of warriors to handle the new threat. Nevertheless, many young men had already moved up the Little Big Horn, working through the various ravines in small groups, attacking the advancing columns led by Custer as he entered and moved down Medicine Tail Coulee. The parties included White Bull, now a noted warrior and war chief. Other, even larger groups, crossed the Little Big Horn directly from their camp circles, being led by Crazy Horse, American Horse, Dull Knife, and others. The Indian camp had been so large that most had no idea that another battle had even occurred, a few men saying afterward that they thought the firing in the south had been caused by hunting parties.

The battle in the low lands across the river from the main village increased in intensity after Reno's inglorious retreat. Lead elements of Custer's troop tried to cross the Little Big Horn near the source of Medicine Tail Coulee, but the soldiers met determined resistance, coming from the central *tiospayes* of the Lakota camp. Rebuffed, the army troops at times seemed to be unsure of their advance, not knowing the terrain. For a precious half hour, they waited for orders, Custer probably trying to decide whether to fight his way back and reinforce Reno or proceed. Perhaps, as one historian has suggested, Custer received a wound here in the coulee, which temporarily disrupted the command.

More likely, the Lakotas and Cheyennes outfought the exhausted troops at every turn. Some troops tried to reach the heights above the draw only to find that Indians from the village had already cut them off. Companies fought as best as they could, working their way northward beneath the eastern bluffs of the Little Big Horn. But one by one, the companies disintegrated, as troopers fell from extremely accurate rifle fire. Unlike the Indians, the cavalrymen had difficulty controlling their horses and shooting at the same time. Many Indians who participated in the battle later said that the "soldiers were easy to shoot, standing straight in the saddle." The troops, on the other hand, did relatively little damage against the relentless Lakota and Cheyenne onslaught. Soon heavy smoke invaded the battlefield, making it even more difficult for the soldiers to identify targets or to respond to orders.

With the troops confused and forced to protect their wounded, many of the Lakota and Cheyenne dismounted and moved up the draws, using the tall grass and shrubs for cover. Ten soldiers fell for every Indian. By afternoon, Custer and his men huddled in two small groups, some six miles north of the encircled Reno, waiting for death. Many of the men were wounded. Some started putting pistols to their own heads. As the many small groups of Lakota warriors surrounded the remainder, the army troops seemed to give up. Custer, and the remanent of his command of 204 men, had their last stand late that afternoon, June 25.

As silence fell over the battlefield, the young Sioux and Cheyenne victors pillaged the saddlebags and persons of the dead troops. They found cartridge belts, often intact, without any bullets missing, testimony to the great difficulty that cavalrymen had in maintaining an accurate fire while controlling their horses. They found carbine rifles, some of which hardly had been fired. They pulled the pants and shirts off the soldiers, leaving them nearly naked in the sun. Clothing sold at a premium in the Missouri River trading establishments and the soft wool uniforms met the needs of the people.

Finally, the victorious warriors collected all the cavalry horses that now ran about unattended. Among them was the sorrel horse with four white feet that Custer had ridden. Several warriors knew it to be Custer's since they also identified the colonel's body. Both the animal and Custer's field glasses had fallen into the hands of the young grandson of the Dakota leader Inkpaduta, called Sounds-The-Ground-As-He-Walks. He and his grandfather had been in Sitting Bull's camp.

But Sounds-The-Ground-As-He-Walks had not killed the American officer. Many years later, some would claim that the coup had been White Bull's, Sitting Bull's nephew. White Bull later admitted that some friends had shown him Custer's body, "lying naked" where the monument now stands. But he seemed uncertain whether it had been he who had killed the colonel. Another possible candidate was American Horse, a man who felt more certain of his role in the fight. But there had been so much smoke and confusion. Many warriors later confided that they were unaware of Custer's presence, even after the battle, a likelihood given the size of the Indian camp.

Back in the village, women and children still seemed uncertain about what to do. Some packed and prepared to leave, whereas others fell into a horrid chant after relatives carried in the bodies of loved ones who had been killed. Although the chanting seemed to grow into the afternoon, the combined losses of the Lakotas and Cheyennes were fewer than thirty men in both battles, an incredibly small number given the extent of the carnage. Sitting Bull tried to convince the women to sing rather than go into mourning. He had little success.

As dusk approached, the huge camp broke into a spontaneous orgasm of mourning and celebration. Dancing and feasting went on hand and hand with funeral preparations. Many women from the camp circles went out to the battlefield to look at the dead soldiers. Some, suffering from grief, mutilated the bodies, cutting off hands, feet, and even heads. But the men did not participate, fearing that the blood from the dead would pollute their war charms.

Another group of roughly twenty Lakota women, headed by Twin Woman, curious and excited, asked to see the body of Custer, the soldier chief. A young warrior pointed him out, lying on his back, nearly naked, but not mutilated in anyway. One of the women, however, walked over to Custer, came astride him, lifted up her dress, and urinated in his face. Twin Woman, who later described the event, swung at his head with an axe handle.[2]

But as the feasting, dancing, and crying went on into the night, the chiefs tried to bring the people back to reality. The immense camp that had formed on the Little Big Horn could not continue to exist. There were simply too many people and too many horses to feed. As news arrived of soldiers on the Little Big Horn north of the camp, Sitting Bull and the other camp leaders decided to move farther west into the Big Horn Mountains.

For his part, Sitting Bull must have been pleased. *Wakantanka* had saved them, as he had promised to do. And Sitting Bull's vision had certainly solidified his position among his people. Even Gall and No Neck now seemed subservient. The only challenge that existed that evening of June 25 was trying to bring the people back to the daily routine of hunting and providing for the camp. This would prove difficult after such a complete and glorious triumph.

---

[2]The encounter is described in a letter of George Bent to George Bird Grinnell, March 4, 1914, Grinnell Papers, Braun Research Library, Southwest Museum, Los Angeles, California.

CHAPTER 4

Escape to Canada

❖
❖

Custer's annihilation shocked a nation. How could it happen? A modern army, well equipped, completely destroyed by Indians and in the centennial year at that! Answers seemed to escape everyone as news of the debacle reached the east. The United States had come to think of itself as an invincible nation, capable of defeating the most sophisticated of aggressors. It seemed inconceivable that a tribe of Indians, or even two or three, could destroy much of an entire regiment of cavalry.

The first reports of Custer's destruction came after lead elements of General Terry's Yellowstone command reached the scene of the fighting. Terry sent a steamboat racing east with dispatches telling of Custer's defeat. The same boat carried some of Reno's wounded. General Sheridan in Chicago could only forward the unbelievable information and try to answer the horde of newspaper reporters who wanted answers. The simplest way to put them off was to exaggerate the number of "hostiles" that the brave Custer had faced. Ten thousand, twenty thousand, no, forty thousand Indians had followed Sitting Bull, the newspapers soon reported. Such a village could place in the field ten thousand men, outnumbering Custer nearly twenty to one, or so the stories went.

But as the numbers of hostiles increased, so did the demands of General Sheridan to deal with them. As Generals Terry and Crook waited along the Yellowstone for orders, Sheridan asked the army and Congress for more men and more supplies. The destruction of Custer had to be avenged, and Sheridan plotted "total war" once more against the Sioux. Virtually every request that the general made was received favorably. Sitting Bull and other Lakota leaders had probably hoped that their great victory had taught the Americans a lesson and brought peace to the plains. In actuality, it only led to a more expanded war.

Over the summer of 1876, Sheridan planned a two-stage offensive. He hoped to engage the hunting bands and disrupt their hunts to the point where they could not prepare meat for the coming winter. This called for the continued movement of troops up and down the valleys where the tribes hunted. For the second phase of the operation, Sheridan turned to the reservations since agents had reported that many Indians had left these havens to join Sitting Bull. Sheridan received the authority to occupy the various agencies with troops and control them by any means. He waited until October to do this, the soldiers disarming all the Indians at Standing Rock, Cheyenne River, Spotted Tail, and Red Cloud Agencies. The army also confiscated all Indian ponies, selling them in the eastern settlements. Without horses and arms, the agency Indians could never again give assistance to the hunting bands.

Once the agencies had been militarily occupied, the debate over the Black Hills could be settled—this time at the point of bayonets. Sheridan's troops simply intimidated the Sioux into signing a new land session. Congress assisted the new "negotiation" by refusing to appropriate funds necessary to purchase food for the Indians, a clear violation of existing treaties. By late fall, faced with starving families, Lakota agency leaders signed new agreements. The government would purchase the Black Hills and the hunting domain to the west of it. Authorities made no attempt to follow the letter of the law, which now required that three-fourths of the adult male population of the

various tribes sign the agreement. That would have made necessary the signatures of Sitting Bull and the others still out. After a few signatures had been acquired, the president declared
that thereafter the Black Hills legally belonged to the United
States. Congress sanctioned the "agreement" with ratification
on February 28, 1877.

Meanwhile, on the plains, the army cautiously pursued
the hunting bands. By July 1876, the Indians who had destroyed Custer had moved into the headwaters of the Rosebud. A month later, they entered the Tongue River valley, pur-
suing buffalo in a leisurely fashion. The hunting seemed more
difficult than years before since the herds had dwindled. By
August, with rations declining, the great village broke up as
Sitting Bull and his Hunkpapas, along with a few Minneconjous and Sans Arcs, turned eastward into the badlands south
of the Missouri River. The dispersal signalized the beginning
of the end for Lakota nationhood.

Crazy Horse, with many Oglalas and Cheyennes, went the
opposite direction, moving toward the Black Hills. Generals
Terry and Crook followed these movements, being unsure of
their ability to deal with the Indians even though their combined strength totaled four thousand men. In effect, Sitting
Bull had shattered the confidence of the American commanders. As the Indians divided, they did too, Crook following
Crazy Horse, and Terry staying with Sitting Bull. But both remained at safe distances.

In early September, lead elements of Crook's cavalry accidentally stumbled onto a small camp of thirty-seven lodges of
Minneconjous. One hundred fifty men, led once again by
Frank Grouard, attacked at dawn not having any idea of
whom they were firing at. As the Indians ran to the bluffs
nearby, the troops killed mostly the old and the young who
had difficulty escaping the carnage. But the small cavalry de-
tachment under Captain Anson Mills had little stomach for a
serious fight, preferring ambush and sniping to all-out assault.
As more Lakotas arrived to help later in the day, including Sitting Bull and Crazy Horse who rode hard to reach the scene,

the soldiers broke off the engagement known as the battle of Slim Buttes. Crook pronounced it a victory, as he was often prone to do, and retired for the winter.

As fall came on, the Lakota hunters faced ever more hardship. Buffalo herds seemed more elusive, even with scouts going out in every direction to search for the animals. White Bull, who had been wounded at Slim Buttes, noted some years later that it was during this fall of 1876, that the hunting bands first encountered the increased activity of hide hunters who had located themselves near the Missouri River trade posts and in the Black Hills. "We discovered that the move to exterminate the buffalo was on," he said, "buffaloes were killed but only their hides were taken and the meat left with poison spread on it."

The slaughtering forced the various Lakota *tiospayes* to separate. The Oglalas under Crazy Horse stayed through much of the fall in the Powder River country, but they moved farther south as the snow came to the plains. After Christmas, the army attacked Crazy Horse's village several times. Thereafter, small groups of his people left, often during the night, to return to the agencies. By spring 1877, the Oglala, Brulé, and Cheyenne contingent of the once powerful hunting coalition could no longer withstand the onslaught of the army and the constant hunger. After Chief Spotted Tail visited the village, over a thousand people went back to his agency with him. Crazy Horse himself surrendered soon thereafter, and during a subsequent scuffle with army guards was bayonetted in the back.

Sitting Bull and his followers undoubtedly heard of the troubles that Crazy Horse and others of the hunting group had experienced. The Hunkpapas and many Minneconjous nevertheless stayed together into the fall, hunting for a while in the Big Horn Mountains. By October, the buffalo had led them north of the Yellowstone River, into the vicinity of growing army activity. A new force had been equipped at Fort Lincoln and sent into the Yellowstone valley to build forts. Colonel Nelson A. Miles commanded this new army of mostly infantryman. The colonel hoped to secure the Yellowstone valley before winter set in, and he had begun constructing a "containment," or unwalled defensive position, at the mouth of the Powder River, in the heart of the Hunkpapa domain. But Miles's plan suffered from a lack of supply since steamboats could no longer ascend the Yellowstone at that time of year. He reverted to using wagon trains, escorted by infantrymen.

Sitting Bull's warriors found the trains easy targets. They attacked the first one on October 11, shooting most of the mules that powered the wagons. They returned again on October 15, surrounded a train of over eighty wagons, and fought all day long with the two hundred soldiers who protected it. But the soldiers held their ground, firing at the Indians from fixed positions. After the surrounded train failed to appear, Colonel Miles marched to meet it.

As the Chiefs' Society debated the renewed fighting the evening before, a growing uneasiness came over the group, which now was dominated by such Hunkpapas as Four Horns, Black Moon, and No Neck. But even leaders like Sitting Bull, who also joined the group because of his status as a *wakiconza*, wondered what the new invasion by the army portended. Would the soldiers simply refuse to leave the Indians alone, and if so, how would they obtain the necessary stores of food to feed their families over the winter?

Fortunately for the chiefs, a stranger had appeared in their camp just ten days before, who called himself John Bruguier. Bruguier had fled from a manslaughter charge at Standing Rock and hoped for asylum in Sitting Bull's camp. Although some Lakotas wished to kill Bruguier, he possessed some Indian blood. More important, he spoke fluent Lakota. Despite making a mistake with Grouard, and being increasingly weary of outsiders, Sitting Bull again proposed adoption, and Bruguier thereafter slept safely in Sitting Bull's lodge.

Sometime, probably late on the night of October 15, Sitting Bull summoned Bruguier and had him brought to the council chamber. Here the chief dictated a letter that Bruguier wrote in English. "I want to know what you are doing traveling on this road," it began. "You scare all the buffalo away. I want to hunt in peace." Sitting Bull demanded that the army troops turn back, then he gave a warning, "if you don't, I will fight you again." The note, signed at the bottom "Sitting Bull," was placed on a stick in the middle of the road where the train would pass the next morning. As commanding officer of the infantry troops, Lieutenant Colonel Elwell S. Otis read the warning, two Indians appeared in the distance with a white flag. Within minutes, Otis found himself facing Sitting Bull and other Hunkpapa leaders who demanded food and ammunition from him. The colonel refused the latter request, but he decided to hand over some supplies. The Hunkpapa then let him proceed.

Within a few days, Colonel Miles intercepted the distressed wagon train. Despite his lack of cavalry, Miles took up pursuit, pushing his men northward even though he must have realized the futility of his gesture. But as before, suddenly two Indians came forward with a white flag proposing a peace talk. They informed Miles that Sitting Bull and other Hunkpapa leaders awaited his answer. On a desperately cold October day, not far from the confluence of the Missouri and Yellowstone Rivers, Miles found himself face to face with the chief, whom he observed, looked rather modestly dressed. Sitting Bull wore only a buffalo robe, leggings, and cartridge belt. He had no feathers in his hair. Fortunately, Miles soon discovered the existence of Bruguier in the party of a dozen Indian delegates, and the colonel pressed him into service as an interpreter.

The talks failed to settle much. Miles opened the debate by accusing Sitting Bull of disliking Americans. As White Bull and other Lakotas remembered the exchange, Miles said, "Sitting Bull ever since you have grown up from boyhood you are strongly against White people." Sitting Bull responded angrily to the charge by pointing out that every time the army came into his country, they came to fight. "And I know you come here again to fite [sic] me," White Bull heard his uncle conclude. As the discussions went on, suddenly it looked as though the infantry troops intended to surround the small group of debaters, prompting White Bull and others to call on several hundred of their own men to prepare for battle. But Miles quickly ordered his men back, and the talking continued.

What happened thereafter is open to debate. Miles later contended that he demanded that Sitting Bull and his people follow him to the new Powder River post and surrender. But the oral accounts handed down through White Bull and others tell a slightly different story. For a time, Miles acted conciliatory, promising food and supplies. The colonel said that the hunting bands could have a reservation anywhere south of the Missouri—a promise that Miles could not keep—if they would just come in. Sitting Bull seemed taken in, suggesting that he hoped to winter near the Black Hills. Miles agreed, even offering ammunition for hunting, an impossible promise. The two sides finally ended the discussion after agreeing to meet again the next morning.

As the representatives of the two sides came together the following morning, White Bull and others noticed that the army troops had readied themselves for battle. Sitting Bull became quite animated. "You are telling lots of lies," he retorted to Miles. "We had a talk yesterday and I agreed with you . . . but now today, you are changed. You are mad." White Bull moved in and whispered to Sitting Bull that it was time to leave. "Now the talk is over," the chief said, "your soldiers are preparing to fight again." Sitting Bull was right. Even before the Hunkpapa leaders reached their lines, Miles opened up. The fight lasted only a short time as the Sioux fled.

While the Lakotas moved north, Miles continued in hot pursuit. Mile after mile, the army trudged on, never really threatening the Indians who possessed horses, but making it impossible for the Sioux to hunt and stop long enough to tend the sick and wounded. White Bull was among the latter group, having taken a bullet in the forearm at the first fight with the wagon train. Sitting Bull then turned south, hoping to reach the security of the Powder River country. As he moved on with

Miles in pursuit, he noticed that his Minneconjou and Sans Arc allies were talking more and more of surrender. The chiefs of these *tiospayes* had advocated giving up at the first conference with Miles and probably hoped that a deal could be made during the second day of negotiations.

Finally, in late October, a large segment of Minneconjous and Sans Arc disappeared from the main camp. Hungry, dispirited, and convinced that the army would simply pursue them all winter, they once again parlayed with the American colonel and accepted his terms of surrender. Rather than guard the entire group of several hundred lodges, Miles accepted as hostage five prominent chiefs, including Red Shirt, Black Eagle, Sun Rise, Foolish Thunder, and Sitting Bull's nephew, White Bull. Miles sent the collection of lodges to the Cheyenne River Agency where the army confiscated horses and firearms and issued rations. The unity and sense of national purpose that the hunting bands had earlier displayed was fast dissipating. Miles, notoriously aggressive, set out to crush the last group of Hunkpapas still out, pushing his troops after Sitting Bull who struck out for the land of the Assiniboin north of the Missouri River.

As one after another of the leading Lakota chiefs surrendered that fall and the coming spring, newspaper reporters increasingly focused attention on the one who would not. Sitting Bull's fame grew with every passing week of resistance. Reporters hounded the army for information. Where was the Hunkpapa who had destroyed Custer? How many warriors were still with him? Would the west ever be safe as long as he remained at large? The army seldom knew. Yet Miles became determined that the chief would one day surrender to him. He drove his troops relentlessly during the winter, even forcing them to march in subzero weather.

As Miles did his best to refuse the Hunkpapas access to the Yellowstone valley, many of the now dispersed *wicotipis* moved north to the vicinity of Fort Peck to trade and beg for food. Nearly two hundred lodges were in the vicinity of the post by November 1. Sitting Bull, along with Black Moon and

Four Horns, were not far away. They never went into the post for fear of treachery, but some of their people undoubtedly did. Miles soon learned of the congregation, and in a terrible blizzard, marched an entire regiment overland from the Yellowstone in an attempt to trap the last of the hunter groups. But the ruse failed since Sitting Bull simply outmaneuvered the colonel. Yet by a stroke of luck, Miles happened on the fugitive John Bruguier at Fort Peck. Miles wanted Sitting Bull, and Bruguier wanted freedom from the manslaughter charge that hung over his head. Bruguier agreed to help the colonel find Sitting Bull.

Bruguier kept his bargain. By early December, Bruguier provided information to Lieutenant Frank Baldwin of the exact location of Sitting Bull, then camped in the Missouri River bottoms not far from Fort Peck. In the teeth of yet another howling blizzard, young Baldwin ordered out two troops of infantry, hoping to surprise Sitting Bull and his people. But the weather turned so bad that the lieutenant marched right by Sitting Bull's camp, and Baldwin's men returned to Fort Peck with nothing other than frostbite. Though Sitting Bull would survive several other narrow escapes from army troops in the two or three months ahead, it became abundantly clear to him and the other members of the Chiefs' Society that the soldiers now patroled all the major river valleys. When spring came, there would be no place to hide.

Black Moon had already arrived at that opinion some time before. Realizing that his people would never be able to sleep well at night under the constant fear of soldier attacks, Black Moon led fifty-two lodges of Hunkpapas north to Canada in late December, camping just west of the Wood Mountains. Major James M. Walsh of the Canadian Mounted Police immediately rode to the vicinity from Fort Walsh, located farther to the west. Walsh, concerned at first, noted that the Lakotas lacked ammunition and were forced to "lasso" buffalo in order to kill them. Many looked destitute, having lost their tepees and camp equipment. Four Horns, tired of fleeing, joined this group with over fifty lodges in March 1877. Over one hundred lodges of Yanktonais soon followed, putting the total number of Sioux refugees at well over two hundred lodges.

The threat of army attack along the Missouri and Yellowstone Rivers had caused this evacuation. But the chiefs also fled out of despair. Many leaders of the once mighty hunting bands had surrendered at the various agencies. Even Crazy Horse did so, despite the knowledge that the army would take his horses and his arms. But the thought of serious resistance to the army faded, as buffalo disappeared, ammunition supplies dwindled, and the particularly harsh winter storms blanketed the plains. As the council fires burned in the few remaining Lakota lodges still outside the agencies, Sitting Bull spoke strongly against surrender, but even he recognized that the kind of national unity demonstrated in June 1876 was no longer possible, and he could see the futility of continuing the war. In early May, with a following of 135 lodges, the chief who had helped bring destruction on Custer crossed the international boundary to live with his brethren in Canada.

In Canada, Major Walsh could easily see the economic despair that existed among the Lakotas. Fortunately, Walsh was a humane person who sought ways to end the suffering of the Indians. Yet the arrival of the Sioux had produced an international incident. Walsh had no assurance that Colonel Miles and his troops would respect the border that separated them from the Sioux. It seemed paramount to Walsh that he convince the earliest arriving Lakota leaders that they stop the fighting. They simply could not stay in Canada for a time, cross the border, fight with the American army, and then return to Canadian lands.

After Walsh's initial conversations with Black Moon and Four Horns, the major seemed reassured that he could handle the situation. Yet in his report, he noted the absence of Sitting Bull, a man whom he knew had much influence. Would the war chief be as pliable? Walsh could only speculate. He had learned that Sitting Bull was merely Four Horn's "head soldier," and thus, might be less of a threat to peace than feared. Yet Walsh seemed to have a considerable amount of respect for

Sitting Bull even before he met the man. Indeed, he seemed to look forward to the challenge of controlling the *wakiconza/blotaunka* who had destroyed Custer.

Likely Walsh's views on Sitting Bull came from a Catholic priest, Father J. B. N. Genin, who spent some time along the Canadian frontier. Genin knew both Sitting Bull and Walsh. In a September 8, 1876, article, Genin identified Sitting Bull as "first soldier to his uncle," the head chief. Although Genin identified this uncle as Black Moon, a minor discrepancy, he did comprehend the difference between hereditary chieftain-ships and *blotaunkas*. Genin also felt that Sitting Bull had the perfect right to defend himself and that the American army had been in the wrong. "If some violated treaty can be pointed to," he wrote, "we would understand it [Custer's campaign]. But no! Not one single case can be brought forth, and I . . . defy anyone to prove that they ever saw Sitting Bull do any mis-chief." Walsh seemed to take the same view, sternly warning the Sioux to obey the law, but showing considerable compas-sion for their circumstances and fully expecting that they would react reasonably to his demands.

Undoubtedly, Walsh's growing sympathy for the Lakotas derived from the incredibly pathetic situation that they were in when they arrived and the willingness of all the chiefs to ac-cept his terms. Black Moon and other leaders told the major that they came only to "look for peace," during the initial council in December 1876. When Walsh told them that the Queen's government would not allow them to come and go, using Canada as a refuge, they all promised to stay in Canada. At this, Walsh said they could exchange buffalo hides for goods, even ammunition, with the local French-Canadian trader Jean Louis Legaré. Black Moon was highly appreciative.

Walsh followed the same procedure with the Lakotas who came that spring. He found Four Horns to be reasonable and interested in preserving peace. Walsh spoke at some length with Medicine Bear, the chief of the Yanktonais who had fled from the vicinity of Fort Peck. Medicine Bear simply said that his people could no longer trust the Americans. This report, filed with Canadian officials on March 15, 1877, again pointed out that Sitting Bull had yet to arrive. But Walsh expected him, reporting again that the Hunkpapa leader was merely a "head soldier," despite his growing reputation in the United States.

Once Sitting Bull fled over the border, Walsh and half a dozen Royal Canadian Mounted Police rode out to see the chief. As a courtesy, the Canadians also escorted a Catholic Priest from Sanding Rock, young Abbot Martin Marty. Marty had come to Canada with a message from the American government, inquiring if peace was possible. Walsh found the chief with over one hundred lodges of people well west of the Wood Mountains not far from Frenchman's Creek. "I was particularly struck with Sitting Bull," Walsh said on coming face to face with him. Walsh described him as a man of "short stature," but the chief had a pleasant face, a mouth that displayed "great determination" and an engaging smile. But when he spoke, Walsh said, "his speech showed him to be a man of powerful capability."

The discussions that followed broached no new ground. Walsh made it clear that the Hunkpapas and the few Sans Arcs with them would have to obey Canadian law. Then Walsh introduced the Americans. Some of Sitting Bull's soldiers had noticed that the two men with the priest had served as scouts for Miles, prompting the chief to refuse to shake Marty's hand. Sitting Bull then made it clear that he believed no one from the "other side," even a Catholic cleric, and he addressed Walsh in a laconic tone. "Once I was rich," he said, "but the Americans stole it all in the Black Hills. I have come to remain with the White Mother's [Queen's] children."

But Sitting Bull still wondered whether the Canadians would let him stay. He coyly asked Walsh if he would let the Americans cross the border and attack his village in Canada. When Walsh assured him of the protection of the Queen's government, Sitting Bull smiled. Walsh then asked him if he had any intention of ever returning to his homeland. Sitting Bull retorted, "What should I return for? To have my horses and arms taken away?" Getting more excited, he continued, "On the American side, I saw they were running us in every direction . . . I saw we were all going to be destroyed." The Americans had lied and cheated the Sioux, and the Indians expected nothing to change in the future.

Walsh came to like Sitting Bull almost from the start. The rumors along the border may have prompted some of his sympathy. His report of June, relayed to officials at Fort Garry, indicated that soldiers within the ranks of Miles's command intended to "kill all [Indians] who talked." Of course, no one could substantiate such a charge, but at Slim Buttes, it would seem that little attention had been given to saving small children. Walsh pitied the Sioux and did what he could to help them. Fortunately, a plentiful supply of buffalo could be found west of the Wood Mountains, and with ammunition available at the Canadian trade stores, the Lakota refugees easily fed their families, at least during the summer of 1877.

But Canadian officials soon found in discussions with the United States that their sympathy for the new arrivals put them in a difficult position. They could always argue to the Americans that they lacked the troops with which to expel the Indians, but such an admission seemed tantamount to an invitation to the American army. And Colonel Miles had made just such a request to his superiors. The Canadian government soon made it clear in diplomatic correspondence that an invasion would not be tolerated. Instead, they appealed to the Americans to soften their terms for surrender, perhaps allowing the Indians to keep their arms and ponies.

Given the recent defeat of Custer, the suggestion remained completely unacceptable to the American government. Indeed, Washington officials countered by proposing that the Canadians disarm the Indians and give them a reservation in Canada. As this quibbling continued, finally Great Britain stepped in to act as spokesperson for Canada, bringing about some diplomatic cooperation. By August 1877, both sides agreed that the Canadians would advise the Indians to return to American soil and that the United States would send a high-level commission to offer reasonable terms of surrender.

Oddly, the Department of War selected the "peace" commission that came together that fall. It included General Terry as head spokesperson, and Albert Gallatin Lawrence, a lawyer who rose to the rank of Brigadier General during the Civil War. Neither had the qualifications to talk peace with the Sioux. But they went anyway, being met at the international boundary by Lieutenant Colonel James F. Macleod, Commissioner of the Northwest Mounted Police. The Mounties and Americans traveled on to Fort Walsh, where they expected to meet with Sioux leaders in mid-October.

Meanwhile, Major Walsh received the unenviable task of traveling to Sitting Bull's camp and convincing him and his fellow chiefs to attend the convention. Walsh knew the job would be difficult, given the tremendous distrust that Sitting Bull had already displayed toward the Americans. It seemed all the more problematic, however, after news arrived of a large party that was approaching the Sioux camps east of Fort Walsh. Although the Indians feared it to be American troops, Walsh assured them that this was not possible. The major rode out to discover over a hundred Nez Perce Indians who were also fleeing American troops. They had been part of Chief Joseph's people, who had been forced from an Idaho reservation. The tribe of nearly a thousand men, women, and children had refused to move to new lands allocated for them and were attempting to escape the army that had been sent to overtake them.

The Nez Perce had created a sensation in the press. At every turn, they had avoided the Americans, crossing through the Rocky Mountains in southern Montana, and escaping troop after troop. Finally, in desperation, they fled north, avoiding the garrisons along the Yellowstone and Missouri Rivers, hoping to reach Canada and join Sitting Bull. Joseph had almost accomplished his task when forty miles south of the Canadian border, not far from Fort Walsh, they ran into Miles who had been expecting them.

The "battle" that ensued was hardly worthy of the word. The Nez Perce were virtually out of ammunition, and they had many women and children. With considerable numbers wounded and dying, Joseph surrendered. Only White Bird and a hundred followers escaped Miles to reach Sitting Bull's camp. They were in a pitiful condition when the battle with Miles had begun, having traveled hundreds of miles, often without food and clothing. Once escaping the soldiers' trap, they had to trudge on into Canada. Many, including over fifty women and children in the group, were wounded, some severely. Even Walsh decried their condition.

The appearance of these desperate and often dying people made Walsh's job even more difficult. Sitting Bull immediately confronted the major. Why, the chief asked, should the Canadians insist that the Sioux negotiate with Americans who chose only to shoot Indians rather than talk with them? "You see these men, women, and children, wounded and bleeding, we cannot talk with men who have blood on their hands." But Walsh insisted and used all of his persuasive influence with Sitting Bull to convince him to come. Finally, after considerable talking, a delegation of twenty-odd men came together, virtually all of whom were war leaders. Though Sitting Bull would attend, Black Moon, Four Horns, and even Gall remained behind. The Sioux representatives promised to see what the Americans wanted, but they warned Walsh not to expect peace.

The two delegations met at Fort Walsh on October 17, 1877. Major Walsh kept careful notes. "There was a doubt at first as to whether the Indians would shake hands with the [American] commissioners," Walsh confided. "But that was soon settled by the entrance of Sitting Bull who shook hands warmly with me, and then passed the Commissioners in a most disdainful manner." Further insult came when the chiefs passed the peace pipe. The Indians shared it among themselves and ignored the Americans. The Sioux expected "lies" from Terry and Lawrence, as they put it, and obviously saw no need to let them desecrate one of their sacred traditions.

In an awkward manner, perhaps symptomatic of the impossible task at hand, Terry rose from his chair and outlined the American position. The government in Washington wanted peace and would grant the Indians a "full pardon." They would be disarmed and have their horses taken away, but the ponies would be sold at auction and the proceeds used to purchase farming implements. As he spoke, most of the Indian leaders sat dispassionately smoking. But as the words of peace and fair treatment were translated, an occasional, rye smile lit up the downcast faces of the Indian delegates. At one point, Spotted Eagle even winked at Colonel Macleod, just to let the Canadian know that he did not believe a word that was being said.

After Terry had finished, his audience greeted his message with complete silence. For what seemed like an eternity, no one said anything. Terry grew restless, as did the Canadians. Finally, as expected, Sitting Bull got to his feet. "We did not give you our country," he began, "you took it from us; ... you think me a fool, but you are a greater fool than I am; this is a medicine [sacred] house; you come and tell us stories [lies] in it, and we do not want to hear them." Others followed, The-One-That-Runs-the-Ree saying simply, "You don't treat us well, and I don't like you at all!" Finally, after the others said much the same, the Indians perfunctorily rose to leave, forcing Terry to painfully ask if that meant that his offer had been rejected. "If we told you more," Sitting Bull said over his shoulder, "you would have paid no attention."

To help smooth over relations with the United States, Major Macleod then had his own council with Sioux leaders where he reiterated the position of the Canadian government. The Lakotas and Yanktonais would have to live off the buffalo, which, Macleod feared, would eventually disappear. They could trade for munitions as long as they behaved themselves, but they could expect nothing from the Queen's government. To this, Sitting Bull and others responded that they liked the Canadian policemen very much and had come to see the Americans only because Walsh had asked them to do so. But they would never go back to the United States. Macleod put this in writing and handed it to Terry as the American general departed the fort.

Macleod took no satisfaction in the failure of the Terry commission. He realized that the Americans probably expected failure. The commission had been put together by the military and staffed with two officers who were ordered not to grant any concessions. The offer of peace had to be made for the sake of saving face and to honor the agreement made with the Canadians during the previous August. But the failure of the Terry Commission had left Macleod with a huge headache—the colonel now had to control several thousand Sioux Indians with a handful of policemen.

Macleod asked for and was granted reinforcements. By December 1877, the force near Wood Mountain expanded from a mere eight men to sixteen, and the Canadians built a new outpost closer to Sitting Bull's camp called East End Post. A year later, twenty-three Mounties staffed the district, and still others could be brought in quickly. But the Sioux and the Mounties got along amazingly well. Buffalo remained plentiful, and gradually, the fear of an American army attack decreased to the point that the various Lakota lodge groups broke up into smaller camps to better facilitate the hunt. Both Walsh and Macleod spent considerable time visiting these camps and counseled peace.

The congenial atmosphere contrasted markedly with conditions back on the reservations in the Dakotas. In a move to facilitate annuity distribution, the government decreed that members of both Red Cloud and Spotted Tail Agencies must thereafter draw their rations on the Missouri River. But they possessed few if any horses, making the move from the interior to the river difficult. Discontent mounted to the point where by spring 1878, small parties of Oglalas and Brulés began to slip away to join Sitting Bull. Among them were followers of Crazy Horse, whose entire band had reached Canada by May. In all, Canadian officials counted over eight hundred lodges of Lakota Indians located west of Wood Mountain by

summer, along with smaller collections of Yanktonais, Sissetons, Wahpetons, and even a few Nez Perces, suggesting that
the Sioux nation would reconstruct itself north of the border.

Sitting Bull seemed to come into his own as a leader of this
collection of people. Canadian officials led credence to his role
as spokesperson by forthrightly recognizing him as such. Indeed, after the flight into Canada, the hereditary chiefs and the
Chiefs' Society seemed to fade into the background, apparently viewing negotiations with the Canadians and the Americans as a military matter. Indeed, when Sitting Bull spoke with
Terry and Lawrence, only members of the soldiers' lodge were
present. Both Black Moon and Four Horns failed to make the
trip. Even Gall seemed to have a low profile in Canada. Very
likely, Gall lacked the diplomatic tact necessary to deal with
both the Mounties and the Americans.

A second reason for Sitting Bull's rising influence was his
growing reputation among whites. Americans knew very little
about the chief, but after entering Canada, Sitting Bull gave a
series of interviews with various reporters. These stories produced a sensation, and the press printed and reprinted them.
Often, the reporters took liberty with the truth, and it would
seem, on occasion, Sitting Bull did his best to provide a good
tale. But from the half dozen interviews that appeared over the
next several years, an image emerged of a man who was big-
ger than life, manufactured from the worship of marshalship,
so common in America, and a fascination with the "savage"
life of the Indian, a theme found in writings that went back to
the Pilgrims.

This "new" Sitting Bull first appeared as reports reached
the press of the failure of the Terry Commission. Newspapermen who accompanied the missions wrote only of Sitting Bull
and his part in the debate. "As I watched the swaying body of
the Indian [Sitting bull]," one reporter started, "and saw his
mobile face light up as he spoke of the great wrongs of his people, and uttered his contempt and hatred for the American nation, I could not but admire the natural oratory which enabled
him to speak so strongly." But Sitting Bull the debater was

matched by Sitting Bull the stoic monarch. "Sitting Bull himself is a man who has but few words to say to traders," a reporter wrote, "and even when he was in need at Wood Mountain the traffic and trading were left to the 'merchants' of his court."

One of the first American reporters to actually gain an interview with the chief was Charles S. Deihl of the *Chicago Times,* who stayed on at Wood Mountain after Terry had departed. In discussions with Sitting Bull held in November, he found the chief reluctant to talk of the one event that Deihl hoped to explore—what had happened at the Little Big Horn. When asked about it, Sitting Bull simply said, "I was there." When asked to elaborate, Sitting Bull explained that when the soldiers came, he was in his tent sleeping. His people awoke him, and he "jumped up." When asked about Custer, Sitting Bull said only that he did not "recollect him." Sitting Bull knew that one of the warriors possessed Custer's horse after the battle, but he offered no elaboration. Finally, when asked if the soldiers fought bravely, Sitting Bull replied, "They did not make a brave fight."

Since Walsh had arranged the interview for Deihl, Sitting Bull probably spoke with the American after much prodding. But this would change as more reporters came and the chief became more accustomed to giving interviews. Late that fall, Father Genin arrived at Wood Mountain and had a long talk with the chief. Sitting Bull had adopted Genin in the 1860s, and the two men were close friends, so much so that some Catholic clerics questioned Genin's sanity. Notwithstanding, Sitting Bull opened up with Genin in an interview and answered many questions regarding Custer. He even elaborated beyond the truth. "Sitting Bull's eyes gleamed at the recollection [of the Custer battle]," Genin reported, and the chief went on to give a detailed account.

This time, Sitting Bull gave himself a much more expanded role in the affair. Although he admitted to sending the women and children to safety as the bullets began to fly, he portrayed himself as the leader who directed the fighting. He even intimated that the Lakota knew of Custer's whereabouts

for several days before the fight and that the camp had prepared itself by placing stakes with clothing attached in the
camp to confuse the troops into thinking that these man-
nequins were people. This, of course, fit with Sitting Bull's vision that the soldiers would literally "fall into camp."

But the attempted ruse of the soldiers—perhaps a fabrica-
tion added by Genin to make the story more interesting—is
the only part of the interview that falls outside what is known
about the event. Reno's troops were depicted as quick to give
up. "These soldiers were not brave," Sitting Bull said, confirm-
ing an opinion given previously to Deihl. Sitting Bull did not
claim to be part of the group that annihilated Custer, but he
did address a growing impression that Genin had given him,
that the press was crediting Sitting Bull with the death of
Custer. "Now they accuse me of slaying them [the soldiers],"
he protested. "Yet what did I do? We did not go outside of our
own country to seek them. They came to us, on our own land
and would surely have trampled down and slain our women
and children." Then Sitting Bull vehemently denied killing
Custer, saying simply, "It is a lie."

Other reporters made the long trek into Wood Mountain,
often stopping first at a Mountie camp and acquiring guides.
The best known was Stanley Huntley who interviewed the
chief in June 1879. Huntley had a reputation as a writer who
often stretched the truth, but he took his afternoon with Sitting
Bull much more seriously than in the past. "I have not killed
the whites," Sitting Bull protested in an obvious attempt to
disprove the growing depiction in the press that he killed
Custer singlehandedly. "I have not stolen horses, but your
people sent the long knives [soldiers] against me. Why do you
do that?" When asked about the Americans, Sitting Bull displayed nothing but contempt for them. "I hate them," he said,
"Do you ask me why? Because I and my people have always
been deceived by them."

These interviews ultimately reached the front page of
nearly every newspaper in the land. Although clearly not a

household name in 1876, Sitting Bull had become one three years later. Yet this depiction of him as the "head" chief of all the Sioux was an exaggeration despite the obvious attempts of the Canadian authorities to make him into an all-powerful chief. Sitting Bull's power and influence remained vested primarily in his position as *blotaunka* and the rights that this gave him to head the *akicita,* or soldiers' lodge. Being at one time a *wakiconza,* or one selected to speak in the Chiefs' Society for all the people in camp, this honor remained only as long as the other *tiospayes* in Canada respected it. During the first few years of life in Canada, the other bands present accepted Sitting Bull as their spokesperson. Certainly, he had no equal when it came to Canadian authorities, not even Gall. But Lakota leadership sprung from so many sources that it was simply a matter of time before disgruntled elements appeared and broke from the main camp.

Part of the reason for Sitting Bull's initial success was his ability to convince the Canadians to open their trade stores to the Sioux. The traders had much to offer, including ammunition and food. One Métis trader who had spent the summer of 1877 at Wood Mountain purchased over $8,000 worth of hides and horses from the Lakotas for small amounts of food and clothing. Cavalry horses taken from Custer's troops were being sold by the dozens. Trader B. M. Kay from Fort Qu'Appelle reportedly purchased a horse that even answered to bugle calls! But Jean Louis Legaré did the most thriving business. He had been trading near Wood Mountain for several years, and he became Sitting Bull's close friend.

Unfortunately, the goods and horses taken from Custer's troops lasted only a short time, and buffalo hides became the standard trade item. Many were taken during the summer of 1877 and sold to the traders for food and munitions. But this soon produced a growing outcry from other Canadian Indians who had often made trips out onto the plains to tap these herds. By 1879, competition developed between the Lakota hunters and the Assiniboin, Cree, Blackfoot, and Salteaux

Indians.[1] The most dangerous competitors were the Blackfoot to the west. With the help of Walsh, Sitting Bull negotiated with them on several occasions, working out agreements to share the herds. Sitting Bull even named his young son, Crow Foot, in honor of the leading Blackfoot chief.

But the alliances and the negotiations failed to halt the continued destruction of the buffalo and the resulting smaller herds that came north each spring for fresh grass. Increasingly, Sitting Bull and the rest of the bands associated with him had to move south of the border to get at the herds, and this brought them into conflict with Assiniboins and Gros Ventres, as well as with the American army. Given the choice of either fighting for access to the herds or surrendering and returning to an American reservation, some of the associated Sioux bands still in Canada saw their numbers dwindle. Indeed, even some of Sitting Bull's people had quietly slipped away by the spring of 1879, heading for the Yanktonai Agency at Fort Peck where food could be obtained.

Sitting Bull responded to this desertion by instructing the *akicita* to prevent families from leaving camp for the United States, trying his best to preserve the vestiges of Lakota nationhood still in existence. The order could only be implemented in Sitting Bull's immediacy, but it did reach the ears of Major Walsh who spoke with Sitting Bull about it in May 1879. Walsh naturally was hopeful that this growing trend of desertion would solve the Sioux problem in Canada, and he pushed Sitting Bull to let his people go. Pressured to the point of fearing problems with his friend Walsh, the chief finally relented,

---

[1]Although elements of a Blackfoot Lakota *tiospaye* often worked with Sitting Bull's people, the Blackfoot Indian tribe of western Montana and Alberta, Canada, were different people, who spoke the Algonquin language. In Canada, the Algonquin-speaking Ojibwas were called Salteaux people.

promising to let anyone leave who wished to do so. Many did make the trek overland to Fort Peck that summer.

But most Lakota *wicotipis* associated with the hunting bands remained camped on both sides of the border and harvested the few remaining buffalo that came north. Occasionally, they clashed with Fort Peck Indians who, in turn, appealed to their agent for help. Finally, General Terry, who had forced Miles to stay south of the Missouri River for fear that he would invade Canada, removed his tether on the brash colonel, ordering Miles to drive Sitting Bull's Lakotas back across the international boundary. Miles moved out in early July with seven hundred men and caught the Sioux butchering buffalo along a small tributary of the Milk River.

Miles's Crow scouts, headed by Magpie, led the assault. This man had a reputation on the frontier for his great hatred of the Sioux and had once boasted that he would kill Sitting Bull. As the lead elements of the scouts and Lakotas clashed, Magpie challenged Sitting Bull. The other combatants moved off to watch. The two men raced toward each other, mounted with rifles. Magpie's weapon misfired, Sitting Bull's did not. The Hunkpapa chief hit Magpie in the head, and the bullet carried away the top of his skull. Just then, the American army entered the fight and opened up on the Sioux with canons. Quickly, Sitting Bull led his people back over the border, surrendering the buffalo herds and much jerked meat. Although Miles claimed yet another victory over Sitting Bull, the Battle of Milk River resulted in fewer than ten casualties on both sides.

The Lakotas fled back to Canada, where in 1879–1880, they faced their most difficult winter yet. The prairies had burned for lack of rain, and the buffalo had simply disappeared. Horses began to die from the mange, a mysterious disease caused by parasites. Other diseases hit the people with frequency, scurvy becoming a particularly virulent problem. By winter, desertion reached new levels as people left the Wood Mountain camps, convinced that they would not survive if they stayed. Some of the Indians became so debilitated from hunger that they could not hunt. Fearing outbreak, the Mounties broke their avowed pledge of nonassistance and handed out small amounts of food. Other Indians survived by eating the meat of horses that had died.

One by one, the various leaders of the *wicotipis* who had supported Sitting Bull departed for the United States. The first to go was Gray Eagle, Sitting Bull's brother-in-law. He had been involved in the theft of some Assiniboin horses, and Sitting Bull had been forced to punish him. Sitting Bull tied Gray Eagle and his companion, Pretty Crow, to their horses and forced them to ride from the top of a mountain to the bottom. As they rode, members of the *akicita* fired over their heads. After the lesson had been administered, Gray Eagle never forgave his brother-in-law. Others followed Gray Eagle. In January 1880, eighty lodges surrendered at Fort Peck. Another 125 came in the next month.

Sitting Bull did what he could to keep the Lakotas together, but the bands had no food and little prospect of getting any. Some young men turned to stealing from gardens to feed their families, forcing Walsh to arrest an Indian from Sitting Bull's camp. The chief, distraught and hungry, tried to overrun the Wood Mountain fort and free his relative. After several days of negotiation in which the barricaded police held their ground, Sitting Bull finally apologized and left. But he turned up at Fort Qu'Appelle a few weeks later demanding that the Canadians give his people a reservation and food. He left with neither. By late May 1880, only 150 lodges of Sioux still remained in Canada.

After yet another summer of often unsuccessful hunts, the remaining refugees had finally reached a point where surrender to the Americans became the only option. As small parties crossed the border ostensibly to hunt buffalo, many families kept going, surrendering to American officials. That October, Gall broke away from the main group and led two dozen lodges south with the intent of giving up. Setting up camp in

the Missouri River bottom near Poplar, Montana, other desert-
ers from Sitting Bull's camp soon joined them. Major Guido
Ilges, who talked with these men, learned that they would surrender as soon as they had hunted out the remaining buffalo
that still lingered on in the Missouri bottoms. But the major refused, surrounded the camp, and opened fire with howitzers.
Rather than fight, the Indians came out with their hands high.

When news of the attack near Poplar reached Sitting Bull,
he fled back into Canada. During the retreat, Crow King, one
of his strongest supporters, departed for the south with some
fifty lodges, surrendering to Major Ilges. Crow King's people
"were nearly destitute of food," when they arrived near
Poplar, Ilges reported. "They had but few horses, they were
half naked, and the cold was excessive." The impatient Ilges
concerned himself little with their condition. He ordered most
of their horses taken from them and then forced them to march
through terrible winter weather to Fort Buford, where Gall
and the other prisoners had already been moved.

Receiving more information, Ilges discovered that a large
number of Sitting Bull's followers had also moved in with the
Yanktonais near Fort Peck. The major sent troops into these
camps and arrested the families without a fight. They too had
nothing to eat and little to keep the cold from their bodies.
Some forty-two warriors were picked out of these lodges and
sent east in the spring. In one of the camps, Ilges uncovered
Sitting Bull's adopted brother, Jumping Bull. Ilges took him off
in chains.

Although Sitting Bull had moved south of the border in
December 1880 to hunt with Crow King, and had just as
quickly fled when word of Ilges's attack had reached him, he
too began considering surrender. That winter, the Hunkpapa
chief had sent a number of his leading men into Fort Buford to
report on the situation. Only forty lodges now remained with
him, mostly immediate family. The group still included Black
Moon and Four Horns, men who had always been adamant in
their support for the Lakota nation and in their dislike and

distrust of Americans. They may have wished to die of starvation rather than surrender, but the majority of Sitting Bull's dwindling *wicotipi* thought differently.

With hunger now a constant problem, a change in command at Wood Mountain only exacerbated the situation. At this crucial point, Sitting Bull's friend, Major Walsh, was relieved, replaced by men much less sympathetic. The new Mounties openly advised Sitting Bull to surrender and convinced him to listen to various emissaries who came in from Fort Buford that spring. Similar advice came from Sitting Bull's old friend, trader Jean Louis Legaré. Legaré had often assisted Sitting Bull in his various trials in Canada, and occasionally, he had opened his store to the Indians, providing them with food.

But the great distrust that Sitting Bull had for the Americans still held him back. He finally decided to send One Bull, his adopted son, and a few others, to observe the situation at Fort Buford. They met the commanding officer at the fort, Major David Brotherton, in April 1881, and Brotherton recognized the significance of this visit and fed the delegation well. One Bull walked through the camps of Indian relatives nestled along the river bottom and saw the rations and the warm blankets that they had received. On his return, One Bull obviously told Sitting Bull what he had seen, yet the general report of the delegation was unfavorable, at least when the delegates repeated it in front of the Canadian Mounties. Some Indians, it was said, had been put in chains, a clear reference to the treatment of Jumping Bull.

Turning again to Legaré, Sitting Bull listened intently as the Métis trader debated with him the merits of surrender. Legaré assured Sitting Bull that the reports of mistreatment had no foundation. He proposed to lead yet another delegation to Fort Buford to see for himself the conditions of the captives, taking along some twenty Hunkpapa men. Sitting Bull agreed proposing in the meantime to travel north to Fort Qu'Appelle to visit with his old friend Major Walsh. While Sitting Bull was gone, Legaré reached Fort Buford and returned.

Within days, he had convinced over a hundred of the remaining Sioux to depart for Fort Buford. The returnees included Old Bull and even Sitting Bull's daughter, Many Horses. When the chief reached Wood Mountain after his visit, all that remained behind were a few dozen old men and women and some children. The cause was lost.

In July, Legaré packed up Sitting Bull and the remainder of his followers and headed the wagons south to Fort Buford. All the way, the chief talked of alternatives. He considered abandoning the train, crossing the Missouri and hiding in the Tongue River valley. But as he looked around, he saw only forty odd men and nearly one hundred fifty women and children. The only leader of note besides himself was Four Horns, and he had passed the age of seventy. Most were incredibly hungry, wore rags, and had few horses fit for riding. Legaré fed them as they inched ever closer to Fort Buford and surrender.

Once at the fort, Major Brotherton greeted them. He marveled at their condition. Some of them had clothing that was falling off their shoulders from the rottenness of the thread. Others had virtually no clothing and nothing with which to make tents for shelter. Brotherton had the men file into a room. He patiently told them that they would soon join their relatives who had been moved by steamboat to Fort Yates, the new garrison that had sprung up on the Standing Rock Reservation. Brotherton assured them that the army would not harm any of them, that they would be united with their friends, and that they would be fed, clothed, and housed.

Sitting Bull listened with a sullen face. Finally, after Brotherton had finished, the major asked the chief if he had questions. After a long wait, Sitting Bull laconically placed his rifle into his son Crow Foot's hand and told the boy to give it to the major. "I wish it to be remembered that I was the last man of my tribe to surrender my rifle," he said. "This boy has given it to you, and he now wants to know how he is going to make a living."

CHAPTER 5

Standing Rock and the Ghost Dance Revival: The End of Lakota Nationhood 1881–1890

❖
❖

As the steamboat *General Sherman* departed from Fort Buford in the summer of 1881, a sadly stoic Sitting Bull looked out from its decks onto the countryside. The Hunkpapa *blotaunka* who had supposedly engineered the destruction of Custer had finally surrendered to an ecstatic American military. But Sitting Bull and the last two hundred followers who had remained with him knew nothing of what lay ahead. Supposedly, the Hunkpapa leader and his people would be moved to Standing Rock Agency, the new establishment built to house mostly the Hunkpapa and Blackfoot Sioux near Fort Yates. Major David Brotherton had assured him of this. Here, the military hoped that the chief and his people would become farmers, perhaps even Christians, and give up the Lakota ways.

The Standing Rock reserve incorporated the old haunts of the Hunkpapa people, including the Cannonball and Grand Rivers. The Grand had been the birthplace of Sitting Bull, and accordingly, he expressed a desire to settle on the river. Whether Major Brotherton agreed to this is uncertain, but the military had assured Sitting Bull that he could remain with his people on the reservation. Sitting Bull did know that his daughter and his adopted son Jumping Bull had settled at Standing Rock after surrendering, and he especially looked forward to meeting them. Even Gall, Running Antelope, Four Horns, and Black Moon lived in lodges west of Fort Yates, and they too would be a welcome sight despite occasional disagreements with the first two men.

On the way downriver, Sitting Bull knew of his ultimate destination. Nevertheless, the *General Sherman* made several curious stops along the way. Landing at the new town of Bismarck, Sitting Bull and his followers soon found themselves guests of the townspeople. Various railroad officials met the boat and offered the chief a ride into town on a spanking new locomotive, designed to ferry freight from the steamboat landing. Sitting Bull declined, walking instead away from the belching engine with an occasional worried glance over his shoulder. Later, the Hunkpapa *blotaunka* dined at the Merchants Hotel where he ate ice cream for the first time, a treat that brought a smile to his weathered face. As the local citizenry gathered around, he demonstrated how he had learned to sign his own name in cursive while in Canada, and his admirers responded by purchasing the signatures at one dollar a piece. Curiously, Sitting Bull found the people whom he once had fought so bitterly now to be friendly and kind.But as the day's events came to a close, the army herded the party back on board the *General Sherman*, destined for Standing Rock.

As the steamboat churned out into the middle passage of the Missouri, Sitting Bull soon became restive with anticipation. He knew that Standing Rock, his new home, lay a short fifty miles below Bismarck. But how would his people receive him? He had gradually lost control over the various *wicotipis* while in Canada, and reasserting his influence on the reservation was likely to be even more difficult. More important, during the last few months in Canada, the male societies that had provided so much support to his leadership in the past had collapsed, the young men deserting the cause sooner than the older ones. Would he be able to reinvigorate the societies on the reservations? Finally, just below the agency, the army had built Fort Yates, the garrison already sporting a complement of troops assigned to keep Sitting Bull's people in line. How would they affect his political role? He did not know the answers to any of these questions.

As the *General Sherman* came into dock near the fort, a new day began for Sitting Bull. As the sound of a military band came out to meet the boat, the Hunkpapa leader could see the small bluffs along the river come alive with Sioux people, all waiting to greet him. Even though the sight must have warmed him, the soldiers, armed with fixed bayonets, kept the crowds away in an obvious display. As Sitting Bull searched for his close relatives, he could see only the anxious Running Antelope, who leaped on board to greet him. Military officers and agency officials considered Running Antelope to be the senior "chief" at the agency, and it seemed only proper for him to greet the party. Sitting Bull stoically shook the hand of this hair coat wearer who had become a collaborationist.

In the days that followed, Sitting Bull was reunited with his daughter, adopted son, and many other close relatives and allies. The army had not lied. They were all there. But the army also had orders to keep Sitting Bull and his followers confined to a plain next to the fort where a makeshift camp had emerged. During much of late July and August, the Hunkpapa leader and his people sat, waited, wondered, and ate government rations while under careful guard. On at least one occasion, Sitting Bull received permission to visit the other villages, now containing upward of two thousand Hunkpapa people, located well west of the fort. There he ate with some members of the Silent Eaters and the Fox Society. But it became painfully obvious that the military would not let him join his old comrades.

Just when it appeared that the entire Hunkpapa *tiospaye* might in fact be united, officials in Washington once again deceived Sitting Bull. While he waited at Standing Rock, orders had been issued to move him and the small remnant of people living with him to Fort Randall, well down the Missouri River, near the Nebraska border. The army feared that Sitting Bull might make trouble, and despite his surrender, senior military officials concluded that he remained unrepentant, determined to maintain as much political sovereignty for the nation and himself as possible. Although Sitting Bull's actions certainly did not justify such a decision, he did have several talks with Major Brotherton, which the major dutifully reported word for word to Washington. In one, recorded in July, Sitting Bull rather defiantly stated his innocence and defended the cause of his people:

> What law have I broken? Is it wrong for me to love my own? Is it wicked for me [to do so], because my skin is red, because I am Sioux, because I was born where my fathers lived, because I would die for my people and my country? What treaties have the whites made that the red men have broken? Not one! What treaties have the white men made with the red men that they have kept? Not one! When I was a boy, the Sioux owned all the world. The sun rose and set on our lands. We have sent 10,000 warriors to battle. Where are all those warriors now? Who slew them? Where are our lands? What white man can say I ever took his land or one penny of his money? What white woman, however lonely, when a captive, was ever insulted by me? Yet they say I am a bad Indian. What white man has ever seen me drunk? Who has ever come to me hungry and gone away unfed?

Sitting Bull took the news of his impending imprisonment with considerable anguish. He bitterly swore oaths at the officer in charge at Fort Yates, threatening rebellion rather than go to Fort Randall. But on September 9, the steamboat *General Sherman* appeared once again and infantrymen, flashing bayonets, slowly and firmly closed the cordon around Sitting Bull's camp and forced the nearly two hundred people still with the chief up the gangplank. For the next twenty months, Sitting Bull would be a virtual prisoner, housed just outside the stockade at Fort Randall. These would be days of monotony and self-reflection, tempered only by the fact that the terrible hunger that had dogged his people in Canada had been alleviated.

All that Sitting Bull could do was entertain an occasional visitor who ventured up the Missouri. He gave an interview to a reporter from the *St. Paul Pioneer-Press* in October, but said nothing of significance. He sat for the German painter Rudolf Cronau who had just completed portraits of many of the leading men still back at Standing Rock. When Cronau finished with Sitting Bull, he asked Colonel George Andrews at the post if he might stage an exhibition of all the artwork that he had completed while on the Missouri. Making over one of the barracks rooms into a gallery, Cronau hung all of his art for everyone to see, including his Indian friends. As Sitting Bull walked down the aisle, viewing the reproductions of Gall and others, he became melancholy.

The next year, Lieutenant A. P. Ahern was posted at Fort Randall and assigned the job of looking after Sitting Bull. Ahern, fresh from West Point, developed a close relationship with the Hunkpapa *blotaunka,* spending many days and evenings in his tent. While Ahern's job included taking roll call every morning—the only real demand placed by the military on the Indians—he became a keen observer of the Sioux under his charge and found them to be admirable people. "The camp, like all Indian camps, was well administered by the chiefs," he later wrote. "The children were well behaved and apparently never needed disciplinary measures. This was due largely to the love of the children for their parents and the profound respect paid the older members and leaders of the tribe."

Despite Ahern's appreciation for Lakota parenthood, he did introduce Sitting Bull to Richard Pratt who just three years before had formed the Carlisle Indian School in Pennsylvania. Pratt had recently received appropriations from Congress to recruit Indian students, and he had hopes of bringing east several young men from Sitting Bull's *wicotipi.* But in the conversations that followed, Sitting Bull responded negatively to Pratt's request. "I have seen the results of school work," the Hunkpapa leader said, "The children who return are not white nor Indian. Nothing is done for them. I love my children too much to have anything like that happen to them." Though Sitting Bull would later temper his views on American education, Pratt left empty-handed to look for other, more malleable Indians.

Sitting Bull did love his family and children more than anything else, much as Ahern had noticed. At this stage in his life, his tepee housed two wives, Crow Foot, two younger twin sons, about four years old, and a daughter, aged ten. Despite this rather large flock, that fall, Lieutenant Ahern watched the arrival of yet another daughter, born to Sitting Bull's younger wife. The parents named the girl Sallie Battles, after the niece of the commanding officer, Colonel Andrews. Tragically, Ahern also sat in the tepee one evening and watched as the child went into convulsions and passed away. "Imagine my amazement," the lieutenant wrote, "to see the tears roll down Sitting Bull's cheeks."

But the confinement and the family tragedy did not break Sitting Bull's spirit. Though friendly to the officer who had charge of him, he demanded to go to Washington and see the president, probably recalling that Red Cloud had gained prestige by negotiation. Both the army and President Chester A. Arthur ignored him. He also demanded farming implements and livestock, but received nothing. Lieutenant Ahern noted the inconsistent nature of such demands given Sitting Bull's continued dislike of reservation life. "The Great Spirit made me an Indian," he once told the Lieutenant, "but not a reservation Indian. I would rather go hungry when game is scarce than receive daily rations and lose my liberty." Despite such defiance, Sitting Bull's public announcements seemed to vacillate between a willingness to try something new and a determined yearning for the old life of roaming on the plains.

While Sitting Bull languished in his tepee at Fort Randall, yet another visitor came to see him. This man, John Poage Williamson, was the son of a Congregational missionary who had started working among the eastern Sioux in 1835. Williamson had other helpers in the Dakota Mission, and they had even opened boarding schools for Indian children in northern Nebraska and on the Yankton Reservation in southern Dakota Territory. Williamson found Sitting Bull somewhat intractable in regard to learning the Christian faith, but the missionary did return several examples of Sitting Bull's ledger art, drawings made some ten years before that fell into the hands of the army. The chief enjoyed viewing the pieces once again—several depicted the heroic deeds of Jumping Bull— and he completed thirteen more drawings to go with them, the collection ending up in the Smithsonian Institution. They all represented his exploits among the Crows and Assiniboins; none depicted the Sioux victory over Custer.

Williamson's appearance presaged a larger project that he and other missionaries had begun. In the same year, 1882, col- league Alfred L. Riggs traveled up the Missouri River visiting various agencies in a search for new locations for mission sta- tions. He found the new Indian agent at Standing Rock, William McLaughlin, to be friendly and helpful, despite his Catholic upbringing. While there, Riggs visited the Hunkpapa and Blackfoot camps in the flats west of Fort Yates, many of these people being past followers of Sitting Bull. But on his re- turn, he traveled up the Grand River and found other smaller Indian camps. Farther south, he surveyed the vicinity of old Fort Pierre, which now was headquarters to the Cheyenne River Indian Agency. Many of Sitting Bull's Minneconjou rela- tives lived along the Cheyenne River—ripe fruit, Riggs thought, for Christian labor.

The largest concentrations of potential converts remained at Standing Rock. Here Riggs left his assistant to work the var- ious clusters of tepees scattered west of the fort. This helper was a Dakota Indian whom the missionaries had named Clarence. He preached to the Indians in a dialect that likely drew heavily from the Dakota language but increasingly incor- porated Lakota vocabulary. For a time, Gall and Crow King at- tended worship, listening intently to the word of the Christian God, orated by a Dakota Indian.

Despite only limited success, Riggs ultimately decided to add stations along the Grand and Cheyenne Rivers. This deci- sion came partly because he surmised that eventually Sitting Bull himself would settle along the Grand River and that this leader would attract a large following. The visit to Sitting Bull's camp by Rigg's colleague, John Williamson, was par- tially to determine the interest of the chief. But Rigg's thinking also was influenced by the growing presence of the Catholic Church at Standing Rock, some thirty miles above the Grand. The Catholic mission already had two priests, and rumor suggested that it would add nine or ten sisters within a few years.

The Protestants moved quickly, their expansion into the Hunkpapa homeland beginning in the fall of 1882. They used a station named *Oahe,* built four years before near the mouth of the Cheyenne River as a training depot. After building stations in the Cheyenne and Grand River valleys, *Oahe* became a boarding school, where the most successful pupils from the day schools received further education.

The limited success of the Protestant missionaries derived from their use of the Dakota and Lakota languages in their work. Indeed, several of their workers were Sioux Indians. Isaac Renville took charge of mission development along the Cheyenne River. Renville grew up in a French-Dakota family in Minnesota, and he spoke the Dakota language fluently. Renville received considerable help from yet another full-blood Dakota woman, Elizabeth Winyan, whose son Edwin also worked at the mission. Elizabeth, who could not speak English, attracted many Lakota women into her circle, where stories telling of the coming of the Christian Messiah became extremely popular. The Protestants, much like the Catholics to the north of them, intended to present the Christian faith to Sitting Bull's people in their own language, occasionally even fitting the gospel into the Indian folklore and way of life.

Other white workers soon settled into the small mission community at *Oahe* and along the Cheyenne River as assistants. They included an unusually strong-willed mission worker from Ohio, affectionately called Clementine but named Mary Collins. After working with Elizabeth and becoming somewhat proficient in the Lakota language, Collins moved north to a station opened on Grand River in 1883 adjacent to Running Antelope's village. Later joined by a mission teacher named George Reed, she soon confronted Sitting Bull with Christianity, for that spring, the army finally decided to release the chief from his imprisonment.

By this time, many of the former followers of Sitting Bull had adjusted to their new lives on the reservations. Major McLaughlin, the Standing Rock agent, reported in September 1882 that nearly all of them remained "honest in their convictions, sincere in their expressions, and anxious to learn." He actually preferred them to old "loafers" who followed Running Antelope, these people being well disposed but "more derelict." Sitting Bull's people still possessed that sense of being "untutored children of nature," according to McLaughlin, and thus willing subjects in the great assimilation experiment that was underway at Standing Rock. They seemed anxious to receive oxen and farm tools and to put them to work. Given these observations, it seemed foolish to keep their leader under guard. Sitting Bull reached Standing Rock in May 1883, somewhat humbled, but certainly less conciliatory than many of his followers.

Sitting Bull soon came head to head with his new agent, James McLaughlin, a man of ability and honesty, but also a man ruthless in his dedication to the assimilationist policies of American reformers. These politicians and activists saw the Indian as an anachronism—noble, interesting, and loyal, but completely out of place in modern, nineteenth-century America. In their view, Indians had to be taught capitalism and the pursuit of individual accomplishment, as well as Christianity. This necessitated the complete destruction of tribalism—native religion, social structure, and especially, Lakota political institutions, the sort that had led to war on the plains. And McLaughlin, who had taken over the Standing Rock Agency in 1881, had already established a host of institutions that he hoped could be used to guide the Indians quickly toward the American way of life.

Initially, McLaughlin set out by encouraging the various *wicotipis* to disperse and select sites for farms. Whenever he found willing participants, he handed out hoes and seed with the hope that agriculture would take hold. But this piecemeal experiment went slowly, and he soon turned to organizing farming districts, complete with "boss" farmers. Such native bosses were selected for their willingness to work with the agent and his assistants. McLaughlin rewarded the bosses handsomely with rations, clothing, and even a few firearms that could be used for hunting small game. Some twenty farming districts had been established by 1885, with a boss Indian farmer heading up each one. Down along the Grand River, this appointment of head farmer initially fell to Gall who quickly became a McLaughlin favorite.

Yet another way to promote American "civilization" came through the creation of an agency police force and an Indian court—institutions completely controlled by the agent. McLaughlin recruited Indian policemen by paying them a salary of ten dollars a month, plus rations, and by giving them badges of honor—soldier uniforms, horses, and firearms. The agent almost always promoted the Catholic faith through these appointments by favoring Indians who attended one of the churches or schools kept by the fathers at Standing Rock. The rewards closely paralleled those given the men selected by the various soldier's lodges to serve as *akicitas* within traditional Lakota camps. But the duties of the police force differed markedly. Policemen coaxed parents to send their children to school, they arrested brawlers, and they broke up traditional dances, especially the sun dance, which the Bureau of Indian Affairs ordered the agents to stop in 1882.

To back up the police, McLaughlin organized an Indian court system, complete with Indian judges. Activity deemed inappropriate could result in a person being dragged in front of the judge, where a fine would be levied, or an individual could even receive jail time. Sitting Bull, at one point, would have his axe confiscated by the Indian judge at Standing Rock after brawling with another Indian. Although McLaughlin seemed more lenient in the enforcement of rules than some agents, he did try to stop dances, feasts, or any tribal gathering that hindered farm work. Of course, the farther that the various, small *wicotipis* moved from the central agency staff at Standing Rock, the more impossible it became to enforce such restrictions.

Even though Sitting Bull certainly had inklings that a new system existed at the agency for creating status and influence within the Indian community, and that the old male societies were being dismantled, virtually on the day he arrived, he demanded of Agent McLaughlin that he be recognized as the "head chief" of the agency. Even Sitting Bull must have realized that the agent would never accept this rather dubious bluff. The Hunkpapa *blotaunka* had long since given up any hope of acting as a *wakiconza* for his *tiospaye*, and he had known for some time that the honor of head chief, as the agent called it, had been given to Running Antelope, who had once been an important hair-coat wearer. Furthermore, the agent had selected favorites to serve in other capacities, including Sitting Bull's rivals, Gall and Crow King.

McLaughlin listened patiently to Sitting Bull's arguments regarding his political position and then denied his request for recognition. Sitting Bull would be treated like any other Indian on the reservation and would have to earn privileges. The agent soon thereafter reported to Washington that he had no intention of recognizing the Hunkpapa leader as a major chief. His description of Sitting Bull ended with a derogatory comment: to McLaughlin, he was simply an "ignorant leader."

An even more serious attack on Sitting Bull's status and position within the Hunkpapa band came that summer when a congressional commission came to investigate the negotiation of a land "contract." Dakota Territorial Governor Newton Edmunds had obtained general agreements the previous year from all Lakota groups in the Dakota Territory. In the "agreement" signed at Standing Rock, the Hunkpapas and Yankton-ais ceded a substantial section of the reservation in exchange for the implementation of a land allotment program.

Increasingly, the concept of assimilation, or forced acceptance of American values and practices, became synonymous with allotment. Under the deal negotiated at Standing Rock, each Hunkpapa family was to receive 320 acres of land, cattle, and more agricultural assistance. But since allotment would take up only a small portion of the reserve, the remainder of the land would be thrown open to settlement, and revenues generated by this sale would be used to employ physicians, mechanics, and other Americans who would teach farming, build houses, and tend the sick. Only a few dozen Indians signed the accord, however, and the Senate refused to ratify it, the old system of treaty negotiations with Indian tribes having been abandoned a decade before. A federal law now required that three-quarters of the adult male population of a reservation sign any new "contract" for it to be valid.

After the Senate had rejected Edmunds's plan, Congress organized a commission headed by Senator Henry Dawes to investigate the way in which the contract had been negotiated. The party arrived at the agency in March 1883. The senators quickly discovered that many of the Indians who had signed the accord had little idea of what they were doing. When Dawes questioned Gall, John Grass, and Running Antelope, all unanimously stated that they had not been informed that the contract involved the sale of land. "Those men [Edmunds and others] talked a great deal, and we were bewildered," Grass said. Although the Catholic Priest Martin Marty refuted Grass's claim, asserting that he was "astonished" to learn that the Senators were questioning Edmunds's agreement, even Agent McLaughlin informed the commission that the contract did not represent the will of the Lakota people.

This discussion with various Hunkpapa leaders was underway when Sitting Bull reached the reservation in May. After McLaughlin had challenged his authority, though, he seemed fully intent on restoring it in front of the Dawes Commission. Called into the meetings with the senators, he vehemently tried to assert his control over the council. "By the will of the Great Spirit, I am a chief," he began. "I want to tell you that if the Great Spirit has chosen anyone to be the chief of this country, it is myself." After crudely accusing the Dawes committee of being drunkards—Sitting Bull strongly opposed the consumption of spirits—he waved his arm, and the other Hunkpapas in attendance left.

The exodus and the charge of inebriation greatly offended Dawes and the others with him. Nevertheless, they proposed one more meeting mostly for the purpose of confronting Sitting Bull. Once inside the agency meeting room, Sitting Bull apologized for leaving so abruptly, thinking that a serious discussion could then ensue. But Senator John A. Logan directly castigated him: "You [Sitting Bull] were not appointed by the Great Spirit. . . . Appointments are not made that way. I want to say further," Logan continued, "that you are not a great chief of this country; you have no following, no power, no control." Finally, Logan spoke of Sitting Bull's new dependent status: "You are fed by the government, clothed by the government and your children are educated by the government . . . and you cannot insult the people of the United States." The senators then walked out!

Despite the bluffs and belligerent words, McLaughlin hoped that this exchange had taught Sitting Bull a lesson even though the Indians had succeeded in postponing allotment. McLaughlin had every reason to believe that the Hunkpapa leader would become an accommodationist much like Gall and the others. It would simply take some time. Part of the reason for McLaughlin's optimism was Sitting Bull's weakened physical condition. The years in Canada had taken much out of him, and the agent could see that he was in no condition to physically challenge McLaughlin's authority.

At age fifty-three, Mary Collins could see the serious decline in Sitting Bull's health when she visited him at Standing Rock in 1883. "He is now partially paralyzed," Mary wrote to her friends back home in Ohio. "His face is drawn to one side and he looks very badly." She asked him about the illness, and he admitted that he could not control one of his eyes, which twitched, and that there seemed to be no cure. The nerve problem could have originated from any of several causes—stress from participating in the sun dance, snow blindness, or even malnutrition. McLaughlin had given Sitting Bull some presents when he had arrived in the previous spring, but he had used everything he owned to effect a cure from medicine men. But "none can cure me," he complained to Collins, "even though they shoot off their guns, beat on their drums, and sing very loudly."

Nevertheless, come the spring of 1884, the chief moved from Standing Rock to Grand River, a favorite and familiar place. He selected a site some forty miles from its junction with the Missouri River where he took up stock raising and farming. For shelter, he moved into a log house owned at one time by his brother-in-law, Gray Eagle, who now lived farther up the river. Other neighbors included old friends and relatives such as One Bull, Four Horns, Black Moon, Jumping Bull, Lone Man, and Bobbed-Tail Bull, as well as a young, dedicated supporter, Catch-the-Bear. Sitting Bull even seemed to make up with Running Antelope, who lived twelve miles away even though he blamed this hair-coat wearer for signing treaties that resulted in the loss of Indian lands. Curiously, Running Antelope's newfound friendship with Sitting Bull hurt him in the eyes of Agent McLaughlin who increasingly promoted Gall and John Grass as the head chiefs at Standing Rock.

As this Sitting Bull community of four or five houses slowly took shape on Grand River, the Hunkpapa *blotaunka* partially embraced McLaughlin's agricultural policies, preparing farm land and trying to act the part of a progressive. By the late 1880s, he had accumulated nearly two dozen horses, twice as many cattle, and a flock of chickens. Though the grain fields never amounted to much since drought dominated the decade, Sitting Bull relied less and less on government rations every year even though the agent agreed to recognize him as the "ration chief" for his little community. In yet another concession, McLaughlin even let him nominate One Bull for the agency police force, and Sitting Bull's adopted son took the job. Such minor recognition brought Sitting Bull to momentarily stop challenging the agent to recognize him as a leading chief.

McLaughlin followed these rewards by providing Sitting Bull with several opportunities to travel in the east. The agent hoped to impress the Hunkpapa leader with the power and prosperity of the United States. Sitting Bull's first trip was a one-week stay in Minneapolis-St. Paul in March 1884, McLaughlin taking Sitting Bull, One Bull, and an interpreter. Here the party stayed in the Merchant's Hotel and created a general sensation among the local population. An article in the

St. Paul *Daily Dispatch,* dated March 14, called the chief the "most famous Indian now alive," and various newspapermen and curiosity seekers followed his every movement.

The hotel set aside a meeting room for Sitting Bull, and the chief daily welcomed throngs of people who simply wanted to see him. He often signed autographs—at one dollar apiece—and he gave interviews. When freed from these duties, he visited several business establishments, fire departments, and even toured the offices of the *Pioneer Press,* where he marveled at the printing apparatus. Indeed, Sitting Bull demonstrated a remarkable interest in technology. He talked over a telephone line with One Bull, which, according to reporters, "broke him all up." He dictated a telegram to his son Crow Foot who apparently had been sent to Chicago for schooling after the family had moved to Grand River. The party visited the capitol building, and everyone began the long walk to the top of the dome. But Sitting Bull developed chest pains, something that he now commonly complained of, and only One Bull gazed on the sprawl of the city.

The trip made an impression on both Sitting Bull and Agent McLaughlin. The Hunkpapa *blotaunka* later spoke to McLaughlin of the incredible things he had seen. For his part, the agent came to realize that the chief was more than a curiosity—he constituted a major attraction that could bring monetary gain. The proprietor of the Merchant's Hotel in St. Paul, Alvaren Allen, had quietly noted to McLaughlin the possible pecuniary advantage of engaging Sitting Bull in show business. While in St. Paul, Allen suggested to McLaughlin that the chief be signed to a contract and exhibited in the east, where large crowds would pay to see him. The agent countered by suggesting that he, his wife, and son join the party as "interpreters," with appropriate salaries. Sitting Bull agreed to the deal after being told that he would visit all the major eastern cities and be allowed to speak with the president.

Sitting Bull had developed an affection of sorts for the gregarious Allen and agreed to perform for him. The Allen show arrived in New York City in September 1884, complete with full runs of lithographs that Allen hoped to sell, depicting Sitting Bull, his family, and a doctored copy of John Mulvaney's "Custer's Last Stand," the "revised" edition showing Sitting Bull standing on a bluff overlooking the fight, directing his warriors. The show, hardly engrossing for its creativity, consisted of lectures on Indian life, orated while Sitting Bull and the eight others with him lounged around near the tepee erected in the background. Nearly six thousand people attended both matinee and evening performances for two solid weeks.

Moving on to Philadelphia, the show caught the attention of a young Lakota named Standing Bear who had been carted off to Carlisle Indian School in 1879. Standing Bear left a vivid description of the show thirty years later, spending fifty cents in order to get a ringside seat. The highlight of the performance was an appearance by Sitting Bull who gave a long speech. "I have been traveling around among you, and I see you are very plentiful," the address began. "I intend going to Washington to shake hands with the Great Father and tell him that I want all my children to receive the white man's education." As Standing Bear heard the words, he came to realize that Sitting Bull had no idea that the show was now moving away from Washington with each new engagement.

Allen then followed Sitting Bull on stage. He gave a translation of the speech, using "great drama" to tell a hushed crowd how Sitting Bull had scouted Custer for days, rushed in on him, and killed him in single combat. Backstage, Standing Bear informed Sitting Bull of the ruse, and the chief demanded to be taken back to Standing Rock. But Sitting Bull's stage career had just begun, for a showman far more imaginative than Allen also had his eye on the Hunkpapa leader.

William F. Cody, or Buffalo Bill, had spent much of his life hunting in the west and scouting for the army. After the buffalo had disappeared and the army stopped employing scouts, he turned to show business, organizing his "Wild West Show," an extravaganza that included Indians attacking the Deadwood stage, gunfights, and even the skill of the legendary Annie Oakley, who shot cigars out of the mouth of her husband. Cody had considerable clout in Washington and by June 1885 had signed Sitting Bull to a contract, paying him fifty dollars a week. Sitting Bull had demanded that the contract allow him exclusive rights to the sale of photographs and autographs, and the total package gave the chief a handsome sum.

Sitting Bull agreed to ride in Cody's show for a number of reasons. Despite his abrupt departure from Philadelphia the year before, he liked travel and enjoyed walking the streets of large American cities. He had also met Annie Oakley at one of her performances in St. Paul and had immediately proposed adoption, giving the young performer a new name—Little Sure Shot. Though Cody received an endorsement from General Sherman to acquire the services of Sitting Bull, the chief agreed to go only after hearing that Annie Oakley would appear on the same stage.

Yet Cody and Sitting Bull became fast friends, the American showman always respecting Sitting Bull and never forcing him to prostitute himself. Sitting Bull called Cody *Pahaska,* or Long Hair, and the scout reciprocated by openly declaring that Custer's defeat was not a massacre but in fact a justifiable defense. Given this amiable relationship, Sitting Bull's role in the gala event—the greatest "western" show on earth—was simply to ride out at the head of the Indian delegation, dressed in simple pantaloons and linen shirt. Occasionally, Mrs. McLaughlin—who again came along as a paid interpreter—would appear with the chief and translate a friendly statement.

Consequently, Cody mainly used Sitting Bull's name, never asking the chief to take part in any of the more strenuous and gaudy aspects of the show. Perhaps the showman realized that Sitting Bull's physical condition precluded such activity. But Cody had brought east an entourage of buffalo, elk, and over 150 horses, all being used at one time or another in action scenes that depicted hunting, steer roping, and of course, the final Indian attack on the Deadwood stage. With a cast of hundreds, the Wild West Show was bound to be a hit, opening in Washington, D.C., on June 22 and closing in St. Louis on October 3, taking in seventeen cities in all. In this short time, the show grossed over a million dollars. Nevertheless, Sitting Bull later returned to Standing Rock nearly broke. He gave most of the profit from his work to street urchins and the poor.

At virtually every stop, newspapermen clamored to interview Sitting Bull. He graciously met them in his tepee, never refusing to help produce the publicity that brought people into the show. In nearly every city, the local newspapers ran a multitude of stories, most being complimentary. In Philadelphia, however, one reporter finally asked him if he ever regretted the loss of life occasioned by the fight with Custer. "I have answered to my people for the loss of life on our side," he retorted, "let Custer answer to his own people for the loss of life." On yet another occasion, he used the interviews to complain of government treatment of Indians and of how the Black Hills had been stolen from the Sioux.

Other unpleasantries did occur. After playing several stops in Ohio, Cody decided to move the show into Canada, where it was thought the crowds would be less animated. Several drunk show-goers had hollered in unison from the stands "hang him," and another assaulted the Hunkpapa leader in his tent, Sitting Bull knocking out three of the assailant's teeth. The daily commotion soon wore the chief down. In a final interview with the *St. Louis Sunday Sayings,* dated October 4, the chief said he was now sick of the houses and the noise and the multitudes of people. He wanted to go home. Buffalo Bill paid the freight in order to ship the chief's prized gray horse that he had ridden in the show back to Standing Rock, and Sitting Bull's stage career came to an end.

Back on Grand River, Sitting Bull settled into a daily routine of tending stock and meeting with the many supporters who lived in the vicinity of his cabin. One of his main goals was to revive the various male societies that had supported him in the past, the Silent Eaters becoming the most useful since it had drawn members particularly from Sitting Bull's *wicotipi.* But the atmosphere never seemed the same, for the senior members of the societies had trouble maintaining control over the younger men who often fell under McLaughlin's control. But young men had to be recruited to sustain the organizations, a fact well known by Sitting Bull.

This lack of respect stemmed in part from the loss of so many important members of Sitting Bull's circle. Four Horns died in 1887, and Black Moon passed on the next year. Increasingly, Sitting Bull was alone, trying to maintain the male societies of the past, the organizations that had promoted him so effectively, without the support of closely related affine kinsmen. Adding to the problem was the fact that with the loss of Black Moon and Four Horns, the Chiefs' Society also literally disappeared. The old institutions that had promoted Sioux leadership in the past—the chiefs' societies and the male societies—simply lacked a role to play on the reservation, for the Sioux nation as an entity had ceased to exist in the face of reservation assimilation.

The lack of interest among the youth of Sitting Bull's *wicotipi* also stemmed from the fact that some young men had turned to missionaries such as Mary Collins. They seemed to be searching for a new spiritual power that could sustain them in the new environment of the reservations. Collins had a two-room house just twelve miles from Sitting Bull's community, using one room as a meeting room. Mary convinced a number of young men to join a Bible society that met mostly in the evening. She provided food for the meetings, and the young men sang hymns and listened while Mary read Bible verses in Lakota. But Collins concluded that one of the leading institutions that held back the Christianization movement was the various dances that the Fox Society and the Silent Eaters sponsored. She lectured strongly against them and found some success at convincing both young men and women to avoid them.

A major test of her success came in the spring of 1887 when the dance season opened. By this time, Collins felt somewhat confident of her ability to keep many of the young men and women from Sitting Bull's camp from attending the tribal socials. "I was anxiously watching some of my pupils to see what they would do," she wrote triumphantly to friends in Ohio. "One girl said to be fond of the dance . . . came up to the mission and spent the evening with me. Two young men newly started in the right way, walked by arm in arm not in party dress so that I might see that they were not going." Only one boy of the "Christian" society attended, and "he is of a poor, low family."

The elders at Sitting Bull's village conferred often with the Hunkpapa *blotaunka* regarding the growing impact of missionary Collins. Sitting Bull's *wicotipi* now consisted of fewer than two hundred people—a mere remnant of what it had been in the 1870s—and within this group, there were only a couple dozen young men. For Sitting Bull to lose any of these meant the complete dissolution of any future Lakota polity. Running Antelope was initially entrusted with speaking with Collins. He pointedly and politely asked her to stop, Collins recording the discussion in her letters home: "He [Running Antelope] says they stay away [from the dances] because they say Winona [Collins] will not like it if they go—so he wishes me to send them." In other meetings that followed, Running Antelope tried to compromise agreeing to let the young men attend church on Sunday if Collins would encourage them to attend the dances. Lakota Indians prayed when they danced and sang, Running Antelope explained, and he wondered what could be wrong with that.

The conflict over dancing soon led to a general skepticism among the elders for both mission and government schools. The missionaries used food to bribe the children into attending, giving them noon meals consisting mostly of cooked meat and crackers. Although Collins disliked this method, primarily because Agent McLaughlin used government rations to attract children into the Catholic schools and the Congregationalists often lacked such a resource, she too rewarded Indians who attended. But the elders in Sitting Bull's camp increasingly opposed schooling because the children, when educated, seemed to give up the "old ways."

Sitting Bull finally decided to approach Collins and discuss church and school attendance. He had visited her briefly when she first arrived at Grand River, apparently bringing in one of his small children for medical care. But he had little association with her for two or three years thereafter. During 1887–1888, however, he went to her house on many different occasions in an obvious attempt to reason with the woman. On his first attempt, Collins chastised him for calling to her from the front of the house—ladies did not respond to such calls—and Sitting Bull cast his eyes to the ground and left. Sitting Bull lacked the "social graces" necessary to speak with this obviously strange *wasicun*. But he came back again and again, one time bringing along twelve other chiefs for moral support.

As the delegation filed into Collins's living room, a confrontation seemed imminent. Sitting Bull spoke first, asking Collins if she expected to stay on Sioux land. She answered "yes." Sitting Bull then said, "shall your horses eat our grass and drink our water?" Collins answered: "Is the grass yours?" Sitting Bull shook his head positively. "Is the water yours?" The same answer came from the chief. Collins then retorted that Sitting Bull's "rain" was ruining her garden and that he should stop it! "For a moment they [the chiefs] all looked at me as if I were insane. Then a smile broke out over their faces and they laughed."

Yet this friendly exchange did not solve the growing cultural conflict that separated the two groups. As the debate went on, Sitting Bull finally compromised to the point where he no longer opposed the education of children, but he deplored the attempts of the missionaries to stop the dances and to change the ways of the Indians. In his travels in the east, Sitting Bull had found the American people to be generally "wicked." "I want you to teach my people to read and write," he told Collins, "but they must not become white people."

To Sitting Bull, this was hardly a concession. He clearly believed that Lakotas must remain Lakotas both in their religious and political practices. Yet he clearly admired the spunk of this American woman, Mary Collins, her abilities in the Lakota language, and the fact that she knew something about medicine. And Sitting Bull knew that learning something of the written form of either the English or Lakota language could not possibly be harmful. He even returned to Collins's house after she informed him that she would not tolerate him smoking in her presence.

But missionary Collins had no intention of allowing Lakotas to remain as Indians. Soon thereafter, she opened a day school in Sitting Bull's camp. The teacher, George Reed, later indicated that for the first year, Sitting Bull did nothing but ignore him. Sitting Bull seemed at a loss on how to deal with the missionaries, their schools, their disdain for dancing, and their demands for cultural change.

For her part, Collins demonstrated both admiration and general aversion for this man Sitting Bull. She often belittled him in letters written for an eastern audience, saying that Gall and John Grass were far superior men. But Collins also noted Sitting Bull's "indefinable power," something that even she marveled over. During a severe drought and with not a cloud in the sky, Sitting Bull announced one afternoon that it would rain. In her words: "He took a buffalo skin, waved it around in the air, made some signs, placed it upon the ground and—IT RAINED."

Finally, after obviously failing to reach an agreement with Collins and her fellow workers, Sitting Bull became more and more critical of Christianity, pointing out its faults to anyone who would listen. "Whitemen [or Collins for that matter] say it is not right for Indians to worship the skulls of buffaloes who gave us the meat of their bodies," he noted retrospectively, "but that we should worship the pictures and statues of

Whitemen who never gave our ancestors anything." He countered the Christian icons by erecting a prayer tree outside his house and attaching to it a buffalo skull, almost as if to match the growing erection of large crosses that was occurring in many parts of the Standing Rock reservation. As the debate with the missionaries and school teachers increasingly reached an impasse, Sitting Bull took the same stand with them that he had with the reservation "loafers" in the 1870s. He openly preached against conversion to Christianity.

This defiance led to several rather humorous indictments of the Christian movement. When asked to compare the two groups, he always gave preference to the Catholics, primarily, as he put it, because the Priests "drink all the wine themselves and do not give it to the members of the church." To his dying day, Sitting Bull saw drunkenness as disgusting behavior. Despite this damning with faint praise, Sitting Bull did realize that missionaries distributed considerable amounts of food to attract worshipers. He once asked McLaughlin how many religious denominations actually existed in America. When the agent guessed about four hundred, Sitting Bull wondered if a minister of "each kind" might "come out here among us." They would feed so many more people.

The Hunkpapa *blotaunka* also enlisted his sense of humor when dealing with the Americans at nearby Standing Rock and Bismarck. When among friends, Sitting Bull frequently mimicked the agent's gestures. He even used ventriloquism to recreate the conversation, making McLaughlin the brunt of the joke. At a diner in Bismarck, he once told some Americans that they obviously thought more of their *witkos,* or prostitutes, than their wives because, he observed, "they dressed them a lot better." This did not sit well with missionaries who heard the story. Collins and others, including Richard Pratt, wrote letters to friends suggesting that Buffalo Bill had led the Indians down a wicked path when they had worked for him. At a similar function, Sitting Bull took the napkin from the table and placed it on the chair before he sat down. Then in sign language, he said to his Lakota companions, "What is good for a Whiteman's face is fit for an Indian's ass."

But the humor did not disguise the fact that Sitting Bull, almost sixty years old in the late 1880s, was losing what little influence that he possessed. At Standing Rock, McLaughlin ultimately recognized John Grass as head chief. More important, the agency police had fallen under the control of men who openly opposed Sitting Bull. Lieutenant Bull Head, who seemed to be McLaughlin's favorite, frequently taunted Sitting Bull when he came to collect rations. Bull Head had it in for anyone from Sitting Bull's camp, even provoking a running feud with Catch-The-Bear. And on more than one occasion, Shaved Head dragged Sitting Bull into court.

The growing factionalism on the Standing Rock Reservation came at a crucial time, for the federal government had become engrossed in a major debate over the future of Indian lands. This debate had led to the passage of the Dawes Severalty Act in 1887, which called for the allotment of reservation lands into 160-acre homesteads—half the size that even Governor Edmunds had proposed some years before. Each head of household was to receive a farm, with the excess land being opened to whites. Congress gave little attention to the fact that much of the reservation land in the west could not sustain farming, and in some locales, including Standing Rock, it took several hundred acres simply to maintain a herd of animals.

Americans in the west quickly saw the potential for the Dawes Act. In the Dakotas, a group of them successfully lobbied Congress to pass the Sioux Act of 1888, which called for the negotiation of contracts to buy up surplus land even before surveys could be run and allotments made to the various Indian families. Armed with this document, the pro-allotment group went to the various agencies in the summer and demanded that the Indians agree to the sale. At Standing Rock, virtually every Indian leader opposed the sale, including John Grass and Gall.

From the start, Sitting Bull opposed the sale of any land. He argued that the Indians needed every acre that they possessed for their children and their grandchildren. At the same time, land-hungry Americans convinced Richard Henry Pratt, of the Carlisle Indian School, to collect the large number of signatures—three-quarters of the adult male Indians—necessary for passage. As Pratt argued and cajoled the various Standing Rock leaders in late July, Sitting Bull organized an opposition camp, telling the various Indian leaders at night that the Lakotas had never benefited from such agreements. Yet during the day, he remained more conciliatory when in session with Pratt. Sitting Bull had learned that if he were to have a say in the councils with Americans, he could not be obstreperous.

For a month, Pratt worked his charm to no avail. The major leaders at Standing Rock refused to sign, and the pro-allotment group finally left for Washington, vowing that they would convince the federal government to force the Indians to accept the terms of the Sioux Act of 1888. Instead, officials in Washington decided to bring a large delegation of Lakotas, some sixty in all, to the capital for a more extended discussion that October. McLaughlin included Sitting Bull in the group, and the Hunkpapa *blotaunka* held a leading role in the talks with the Secretary of Interior.

Sitting Bull remained surprisingly conciliatory in these debates. Ultimately, the two parties concluded that the required number of Indians would sign an agreement in which the government paid $1.25 an acre for excess land after the implementation of allotment. Though Sitting Bull seemed to agree to this, he apparently understood that such a deal, were it to be consummated, could be completed only on the reservation where the signatures had to be acquired. And later evidence indicates that he intended to oppose this with all of his might.

Overjoyed, Congress passed a second Sioux Act in 1889, in which excess land would be purchased. The Secretary of Interior selected General George Crook to head up the commission that put this proposal before all the Sioux people that summer.

At Standing Rock, however, Crook soon faced a wall of opposition. Obviously, Sitting Bull fully comprehended that the signed agreement in Washington had nothing to do with a final contract, which had to be signed by three-quarters of the adult males. He vehemently opposed the final deal despite the agreed-on price for the land. But Crook came to the table much better prepared than Pratt. Even McLaughlin, who had remained less supportive of the initial 1888 agreement, strongly supported this one. He lobbied many tribal leaders, promising jobs and houses, and enlisted the aid of Catholic missionaries at the agency to do the same.

Sitting Bull tried his best to counter the efforts of the agent. He laughed at the promises made to Gall, John Grass, and others. He also brought together the Silent Eaters and harangued them well into the night. "They [the *Wasicuns*] want us to give up another chunk of our land," Sitting Bull told his fellow Silent Eaters, "they will try to gain possession of the last piece of ground that we possess. Have we ever set a price on a piece of our land and received such a value?" Everyone with him that night answered a resounding "No." To invigorate the Silent Eaters and attract other support, Sitting Bull rode around the camp late that evening singing, "The Nation named me, So I shall live courageously."

The next day, McLaughlin used the Indian police to put large numbers of Hunkpapa and Blackfoot Sioux in line and run them by the signing table. An outraged Sitting Bull, seeing the process begin, led two dozen mounted Silent Eaters into their midst, trying to force them back. But Lieutenant Bull Head regained control of the ground and a mixture of Hunkpapa, Blackfoot, and Minneconjou men continued to go by the table, placing an X on a paper that most of them did not understand. In the end, besides the malleable John Grass and Gall, even several Sitting Bull supporters agreed to the contract, including Catch-the-Bear and One Bull. Later, One Bull indicated that he feared that if he refused to sign, he and his family would be cut off from annuity payments, or worse, from the monetary benefits to come from the land sale. The power of the male societies had been broken forever, and Sitting Bull could not even count on his own closest relatives to resist the division of the reservation.

As Crook triumphantly returned to Washington with signed contracts from all the Sioux reservations, most reformers and their congressional supporters concluded that they had solved the "Indian problem" in America. The Indians, they felt, would quickly become self-supporting farmers. Given this incredibly naive view, Congress cut the appropriations for annuities that fall, believing it to be unnecessary to provide the Indians with food annuities any longer. Far worse, in February 1890, the president decreed that the excess land purchased from the Sioux could be opened even before the region was surveyed. The Indians had not been assigned their allotments, and those Indian families living in the ceded land would simply have to move even though the commissioners had promised that they could take allotments where they lived.

As the Hunkpapa people looked to the spring of 1890, they had many troubling concerns. The land issue remained unresolved, no one really knowing what would happen next. The stinginess of the government and its ration plan became more apparent as the government warehouses of Agent McLaughlin became bare. Finally, the drought of the middle decade continued unabated despite Sitting Bull's powers. Hot winds blew down on the prairie during that spring, wilting the grasslands that fed reservation stock and ruining the seedlings of yet another crop.

These signs had not surprised Sitting Bull. He had predicted that the government would not live up to the promises. He had also warned his friends of the coming dry spell. But for the most part, he returned to Grand River and reimmersed himself in the life of his family. He even agreed to send several of his children to the day school at his camp. The Hunkpapa *blotaunka* avoided Agent McLaughlin whenever possible and seldom traveled much beyond the confines of his own small community. He spent most of his time with the dozen or so members of his beloved Silent Eaters.

The only excitement along Grand River came in the form of the extended visit of a New York widow named Catherine Weldon. Connected to the more radical Indian Defense Association, this liberal reformer recently had dedicated her life to helping Sitting Bull and his people, a noble but pretentious cause. In a typical display of generosity, Sitting Bull asked her to move into his house! Rather astonishingly, she agreed. Sitting Bull seemed flattered; the local *wasicun* citizenry was at the same time mystified and outraged. Though Weldon denied any wrongdoing, and McLaughlin failed to find any proof of her immorality, the local press dubbed her "Sitting Bull's White Squaw." Weldon spent the summer ignoring the ugly rumors and painting Sitting Bull's portrait.

Despite the concerns of the local townspeople in Bismarck, Weldon's influence was passive in comparison to the disruptive force that hit the reservation that fall. Some years before in far-off Nevada, a Paiute religious leader named Wovoka had a vision. He had seen the coming of a new era, in which the world would rid itself of the *wasicuns* and put in their place all Indians who had once walked the earth. In order to feed such a multitude, the buffalo, deer, and elk would return since, as he said, they had simply gone into the ground. Some believers thought that this would all occur in the spring of 1891.

Although not a threatening vision, Wovoka's words promised a revitalization of the Indian race. The Paiute prophet preached that such a coming could occur only if the Indian nations then on earth danced the ghost dance, a ritual that he personally would teach, and sang the appropriate songs. Word of this great event spread across much of North America, reaching Indian nations that often were suffering general dispair in the wake of the federal government's assimilation program.

The rumors of Wovoka's teachings reached the Dakota reservations in 1889, prompting several Lakota Indians from Pine Ridge to travel west in search of the prophet. When they found him, they became instant converts, concluding that this man was the true messiah, sent to Indians to save them from the *wasicuns*. This messiah promised a whole new life, one free of hardship and disease, and especially free of the Americans. But most important, if one believed, departed relatives and friends would all return, when the Lakotas danced and prayed. Some Indians started dancing that summer.

One of the Lakota travelers was a Minneconjou from Cheyenne River named Matowanahtake, or Kicking Bear. Weldon, still living in Sitting Bull's house, identified him as being a nephew of the Hunkpapa *blotaunka*, likely born to one of his sisters. On October 9, 1890, Sitting Bull invited Kicking Bear to his camp to explain the new faith and to teach the ghost dance. As Weldon put it, Kicking Bear claimed *"to have spoken to Christ,* who is again upon the earth." Sitting Bull listened intently as Kicking Bear described the new belief.

Kicking Bear unveiled an amazing story of the coming of the messiah. The apocalypse would occur in the form of a flood, and as Kicking Bear explained, only those Indians "who wear the eagle down" would be saved.[1] But a series of other rituals and symbols came with the dance that ensured eternity. Each dancer was to wear a ghost shirt, covered with various designs. The skull of the buffalo took a prominent place on the shirt, this sign representing the guarantee of the animal's return. The sun, the moon, the stars, and even such natural phenomena as rain and hail were often depicted in various fashions on shirts. Finally, virtually all shirts had black eagle wing feathers attached to each shoulder, supposedly necessary to lift the wearer above the ground when the flood came.

Symbolically, the shirts displayed the theology of the new religion. Yet they also represented the militant side of the new belief. For everyone on the reservations realized that the new dance was sure to be outlawed by the agents and suppressed. To deal with this threat, Kicking Bear and others came to ascribe mystical powers to the shirts; they would repel bullets.

---

[1] Another version of the story related by Agent McLaughlin in a letter dated October 17, 1890, suggests that the Great Spirit would cover the earth with a layer of sod, smothering all the whites.

This notion of being bullet-proof was not new to the Sioux, for the idea had been pushed by some *wicasa wakans* in years past when fighting against the American soldiers. The belief had been adopted as much for the expediency of it as for any other reason. The Lakotas always knew that the American soldiers would have plenty of ammunition, and the only way their warriors could compensate for such a deficiency was by finding *wicasa wakans* who had charms that protected them from bullets.

Although various aspects of the ghost dance religion relied heavily on the invading Christian faith—especially the coming of the messiah—in actual practice the ghost dance came to mimic the sun dance of old. Sitting Bull's prayer tree located in the center of his camp became the focal point of the dance. Brush was used to form barriers that defined the arena. Similar to the sun dance, the village selected a *wicasa wakan* to act as dance leader. At Sitting Bull's camp, this honor fell to Bull Ghost.

By mid-October, the ghost dance reached an emotional high at Sitting Bull's village with several hundred dancers coming and going, some participating in the dance and others simply watching. Nearly all these people had pitched their tents on the flat of the river near the dance circle. They all seemed to be searching for something new, spiritually and emotionally, that might help revive the sense of nationhood that seemed so completely lost. Nearby, Sitting Bull had erected his own tepee to use as a command center. The dance soon reached a fervor pitch, going on hour after hour and day after day. Though it was not June—the time of the sun dance— Sitting Bull promised that the weather would remain mild and that his people could dance all winter. The weather held, and the dance went on.

The most evangelical aspect of the spiritual renaissance of the ghost dance was the tendency of dancers to eventually fall into a trance. This happened in a fashion similar to that of the sun dance, with dance leader Bull Ghost appearing in front of selected participants and waving an eagle feather stick in their faces. As the dancers individually fell, they were carried to a tepee—often Sitting Bull's—and wrapped in a white sheet. As they opened their eyes again, they found eagle down on their hands and face. More important, they had experienced visions.

The visions followed one familiar theme—the dancers almost always saw their long departed relatives and spoke with them. White Hand Bear "fainted and saw grandfather who told him to keep dancing." In an unusual break with the past, women joined the dances, methodically moving around the prayer tree, hoping for a vision. When they fainted, many saw their lost children, who, they believed, would soon join them on earth. Soon, individualized ghost songs became part of the dance. Bob Tail Bull, an elder and strong supporter of Sitting Bull, sang, "Look at me, my father has said, you all shall live, you all shall live." The dancing attracted all kinds, even a few policemen. Within days, it had brought the civilization program to a halt on Grand River. Children left school, and men abandoned their farms.

At its height in late October, Sitting Bull offered his prestige to the dance by donning a ghost shirt and entering the arena. He looked splendid. His shirt had a sacred red cross painted between the shoulder blades, here and there observers noted black stars, a blue-black moon, and the down of the eagle. He carried his medicine bag, which had a little feather attached to the end. And his face was aglow with paint, rainbows extending from the outer eyebrows, a moon on one cheek and a star on the other. The sight of his uncle dancing with others was too much for One Bull, who left the police and briefly joined the dance.

At this time, the movement among the Hunkpapa was mostly confined to Sitting Bull's camp on Grand River. But by late October, it spread to other locales, including Flying Bye's village, not far from Collins's house, and another encampment on Live Oak Creek, a tributary of the Missouri River running fifteen miles north of Sitting Bull's house. At Live Oak Creek, the prayer tree was filled with small pieces of rages, representing the prayers of the people. A few policemen joined the dance at Live Oak Creek, and McLaughlin promptly removed them from the roster. Gall finally stopped the dance in this locality in November.

Many who watched the ghost dance and Sitting Bull's participation in it would later speculate about his motives and the degree to which he had committed himself to this new religion. Some previous historians have suggested that he used the movement for political gain. Missionary Collins seemed certain of this, even reporting in early December that Sitting Bull had as much told her that he needed the movement to maintain his position in the Lakota society. Yet Collins lacked anything approaching objectivity in her assessment of the movement.

One eyewitness, Robert P. Higheagle, concluded thirty years later that Sitting Bull had joined the dance because it was his duty as leader of his *wicotipi*. Certainly the fact that a relative, Kicking Bear, had brought the dance to his camp prompted him to give it more serious consideration. George Reed, the Congregational teacher at Sitting Bull's camp, later noted that the Hunkpapa *blotaunka* recognized that the dancing had closed the schools and churches and that this had likely reinvigorated the male societies. Given McLaughlin's treatment of Sitting Bull and the chief's failure to stop the land sale, Sitting Bull undoubtedly saw the dance as a means to hinder the civilization program.

Other whites and Indians also spoke with Sitting Bull during the height of the dancing, and their reports indicate that the chief had a very strong interest in seeing the new revelation through to the end. At one point, a Catholic priest seemed to convince him that the dead could not come back to life. But soon thereafter, he responded defiantly to several policemen: "I want to find out myself whether this is true or not." If anything ought to be stopped, he pointed out, it was the "Christian churches." To the end, in public statements, Sitting Bull maintained a strong belief in his own religion and the ghost dance that it had spawned, and he rejected Christianity.

In an ironic sense, the Christian missionaries inadvertently brought a considerable degree of credibility to the ghost dance. Many of Sitting Bull's closest relatives had read extensively in the Bible by this time, and most had developed some understanding of Christian doctrine, even if it made little sense to them. The Protestant missionaries in particular had emphasized millennialism, a demanding concept in itself and even more difficult to comprehend when translated into the Lakota language. Confusing matters more, the Protestants had tried to draw careful analogies that placed the second coming of Christ into the context of Indian culture.

The first indication of how the Lakota comprehended this came during a "revival" that occurred at Collins's mission near Running Antelope's village during the spring of 1889. Church attendance doubled and, at times, tripled as the missionaries used gospel singing and preaching to attract a large following. The most adamant new convert was Wakutemani, a young man who had fought side-by-side with Sitting Bull at the Little Big Horn. White Sitting Buffalo, Many Bulls, and Little Eagle—all young men from Sitting Bull's band—embraced Christianity as well, as fifteen young people asked for admission to communion in May. These men and women agreed to disavow dancing, or any "heathenistic" practice and to work to stop polygamy, a marriage practice that Agent McLaughlin had recently outlawed. Even Running Antelope agreed with this last proposal, the chief at times showing more consideration for the views of Collins than for his new mentor, Sitting Bull.

Still, Collins felt somewhat perplexed by the views that many Lakota Indians, even her converts, held toward Christianity. At times, it seemed to be a mixture of Christianity and, what was to her, paganism. At the height of her "revival," one future convert related to her that when he was a child, his father had told him that "by and by the Great Spirit would bring forth a daughter who should restore the Dakotas to all their former glory." Athough Collins concluded from this that the

Christian message was getting through, it seemed at times to be quite garbled. "They tell various stories," she finally conceded, "but so much of the Bible is mixed in that it is hard to separate the old legend from new truths."

For some prospective Hunkpapa converts, the Christian story seemed more clear but still confusing. Little Wound, for example, told Collins that he understood that the white man had "got off the right road," and that the Great Spirit had sent his son to help them. "He lived with them for thirty winters and worked hard to help the White Man." But they denied him and killed him, and as he died, it was promised that he would return again to save the whites. Little Wound could only wonder why the whites initially had killed the Great Spirit's son, for if he had sent his son to the Indians, they would have honored him and listened to him.

It is uncertain whether the revitalization at Sitting Bull's camp represented the Lakota ghost dance experience in general—dancing occurred at most of the Dakota reservations—but there is little doubt that Sitting Bull came to believe in the new, hybrid religion as it developed in October. For him to deny the dance, its obvious vision quest, and its powers of transformation, was to deny the foundation of his entire religion. Time and again, he had displayed an unwillingness to do this. And the dance came to represent the last vestige of Lakota sovereignty and national identity. Though political independence had for the most part been relinquished, Sitting Bull and others simply refused to give up hope in the idea of the Lakota nation, even given the fact that most of the people on the reservations had not embraced the ghost dance and many deplored it.

Sitting Bull stayed close to the dance circle, watching with great anticipation as individuals went into orgasmic trances. When a dancer fell, he would wait patiently until the individual revived and then inquire about the vision. He obviously believed in the reports that he received since he had received such visions himself. Yet by November, Sitting Bull stopped dancing and simply watched. Some policemen saw this as a sign that he might be backsliding. But when questioned, he replied that he had a "right to believe what he wanted to."

Probably the best observer of the movement, however, remained Mary Collins who went frequently to Sitting Bull's camp and received constant reports from George Reed, the Congregational teacher there. By mid-October, she found that many dancers seemed to be coming and going at Sitting Bull's camp, some obviously spreading the belief to other locales where dancing was underway and being reassured by Sitting Bull of the viability of the new faith. Many rode in greatly excited, exclaiming, "I saw your father out in the White mountains, risen from the dead." Such news greatly excited the people.

Collins believed that Sitting Bull manipulated this resurrection mania. "He told them [the people] that the Christ had come for the Indians but not for the White people." The Indians, he continued, "would all rise from the dead but that the white people would not and that soon all the land would again be as in the time of their fathers." Any Indian who rejected the message, Sitting Bull argued, would be turned into a dog.

Although Collins tried to talk the chief into abandoning such rhetoric, she failed. For Sitting Bull, it would seem, Wovoka's teachings meshed very well with the general knowledge of Christianity that had become commonplace on the reservation by the late 1880s. Sitting Bull saw nothing wrong with using such knowledge and even displayed a red cross prominently on the chest of his ghost shirt, a clear indication of the dual nature of the ghost dance philosophy. And when young dancers came into the chief's tent to be painted, Sitting Bull etched crosses on their cheeks, noses, and foreheads.

Unfortunately, Agent McLaughlin saw the dance in a much different light. It disturbed the tranquility of his agency and affected the civilization program. But the fact that the dance actually began at Sitting Bull's village only convinced

McLaughlin of the need to act more quickly, for the agent had become considerably disturbed with Sitting Bull's behavior after the land contract episode. He even had queried the Indian Bureau for permission to have Sitting Bull removed from the reservation well before the arrival of Kicking Bear and the dance.

Conflict over land, growing cultural schisms, political jealousies, and the upheaval caused by the ghost dance itself led the agent to more drastic measures. At least one former policeman, Grasping Eagle, later indicated that McLaughlin had considered the need "to kill Sitting Bull" in a meeting with several policemen on August 10, two months before the dancing began. But a plot never materialized. After McLaughlin sent several policemen out to Sitting Bull's camp to stop the ghost dance on October 10, however, and they failed, the agent apparently reconsidered the option of having the Hunkpapa *blotaunka* killed.

McLaughlin's first chance came when Sitting Bull left his village to drive Catherine Weldon to the Missouri River to catch a steamboat on October 22. Weldon had given up trying to stop the ghost dance. In an unusual letter, written just five days before this trip to the commissioner of Indian Affairs, McLaughlin castigated Sitting Bull. He was a coward, a liar, an opponent of civilization, and a polygamist. The letter justified what must have been an anticipated decision—Shaved Head, Bullhead, and Red Tomahawk, all members of the police force, laid in ambush for Sitting Bull along the road to Fort Yates. But the Hunkpapa *blotaunka* took Weldon another way. When Sitting Bull later learned of the plot through Grasping Eagle, he stopped going to the agency entirely, fearing for his life.

McLaughlin's troubles increased by early November when conditions deteriorated at other Sioux reservations. The agent at Pine Ridge had lost control of his people, and conditions at Cheyenne River seemed nearly as problematic since large collections of Lakotas attended the ghost dances and abandoned the government schools and farms. These agents, rattled and unsure of themselves, sent numerous appeals for help and suggested that an Indian outbreak was imminent. The secretary of interior turned the reservations over to the army on November 14. Thereafter, the agents would answer to the local military officials. In a final attempt to calm the situation, McLaughlin visited Sitting Bull's camp on November 17. He found the settlement in near chaos, with men and women dancing, falling to the ground in trances, and reviving to tell of talking with dead relatives.

Moving across the river to camp, McLaughlin saw Sitting Bull the next morning and tried to talk him into abandoning the dance. The agent turned on the charm, reminding Sitting Bull of his imprisonment at Fort Randall. McLaughlin now claimed that he had convinced the army to release the chief in 1883. But when reproaching Sitting Bull for leading what McLaughlin perceived to be an obviously false religion, the Hunkpapa *blotaunka* expressed a strong belief in the ghost dance and the new messiah. He even proposed to McLaughlin that they both go west to meet the messiah and see together if he were not the true savior of the Indian race. The agent laughed at the suggestion, declaring that it would be like trying to "catch the wind."

Back at Standing Rock, McLaughlin revamped his police force, issuing a circular that called for the addition of forty new members. Although the agent attempted to lure some ghost dancers into the force, he soon gave up and allowed Bull Head to handpick the men. By early December, the force had established a base camp just north of Sitting Bull's camp and had sent spies into the community. In the meantime, McLaughlin wrote several reports to Washington officials in which he asked for permission to arrest the chief, intending to use the Indian police rather than military troops.

At that particular time, Washington officials seemed much less concerned with Standing Rock than with the events underway at Pine Ridge. Once army troops arrived in the vicinity of that agency on November 20, several thousand dancers abandoned their homes and fled inland. Kicking Bear from

Cheyenne River and Short Bull from Rosebud seemed to be the key instigators. They took up a position in rugged badlands northwest of the agency, a region known as the "stronghold," and here they danced day and night. As McLaughlin heard the distressing news from the south, he fully realized that the stronghold would offer a refuge for Sitting Bull and his dancers, an event that he wished to prevent at all costs. If the Hunkpapas fled, it would show that he was unable to control his reservation. Again he asked for permission to arrest the dancers, and again he was denied.

Given the atmosphere of mass hysteria that the agents complained of in their reports to Washington, it seemed only natural that newspapers would pick up on the story. Some did, and reports soon circulated of unrest and possible upheaval. Settlers reportedly called for army troops to protect them. Nevertheless, there had been no clashes either with civilians or with army troops. The dancers at Pine Ridge had simply moved to an isolated portion of the reservation rather than become involved in a confrontation.

In addition, missionaries and even some military officers viewed the ghost dance as a rather harmless expression that would soon burn itself out. Thomas Riggs traveled throughout the various reservations in November and reported to his brother that though the dance was having "as enthusiastic a run as would satisfy the most authentic play actor," it had caused no harm other than "to the Indians themselves," that harm coming in the form of their abandonment of schools. In yet another letter of December 13, Riggs said simply, "I have seen nothing in it beyond some rather fanatical dancing and the natural turn the wilder fellows have taken to revive old customs and life." The more progressive Indians had rejected the dance, and most of the white farmers who bordered the reservations were busily gathering their crops.

While the crisis created by the agents escalated, Buffalo Bill Cody rode into Standing Rock Agency on November 28, armed with an order from General Miles. During a friendly lunch in Chicago, Cody had talked the general into letting him bring in Sitting Bull. The orders were carte blanche, even directing the post commander, Lieutenant Colonel William F. Drum, to provide transportation. McLaughlin was dumbfounded and plotted to stop Cody. He delayed the showman for sometime, convinced the post military officers to keep Cody entertained in the officer's club with strong drink—a rather easy task—and then found a guide that led the inebriated Buffalo Bill in the wrong direction. Meanwhile, he hurriedly telegraphed the secretary of interior asking that the orders be revoked. The War Department complied, and Cody went home without seeing his old friend Sitting Bull.

The distraction bothered McLaughlin who increasingly wished to solve this problem himself. As he watched and waited for the next turn of events, suddenly the news worsened. Sitting Bull had received word in early December that "God was to appear at Pine Ridge." He would come to the dancers in the stronghold, so reported Short Bull and Kicking Bear. Bull Ghost had jubilantly informed the policeman Bull Head of this exciting news, and it had been relayed to the agent. But to allay McLaughlin's fears, Sitting Bull dictated a long letter to him, dated December 11, telling him of this new event and asking permission to go witness it. "Today our father is helping us Indians, so all Indians believe," he began. "So all Indians pray to God for life, and try to find out a good road . . . this is what we want."

Sitting Bull felt obligated to go to Pine Ridge and see the new messiah. But he openly feared what the agent would do, and he knew that he needed permission to travel. "I wish no one to come to me with gun or knife," he wrote. But Sitting Bull had received permission to travel to other agencies in the past, and despite the ghost dance crisis, he apparently felt that the agent would relent. McLaughlin neither understood, nor approved, and feared that Sitting Bull and his followers would flee to the stronghold at Pine Ridge. Worse, a day later, McLaughlin's spies informed him that Sitting Bull intended to leave soon with or without the agent's permission.

On the same day that Sitting Bull's letter arrived, Colonel Drum finally received orders to arrest Sitting Bull. The situation on the southern reservations had reached a point where the army had brought in several thousand troops, intent on stopping the dancing and arresting the instigators. Although McLaughlin had been ordered to assist the military, Colonel Drum had complete confidence in the agent and agreed to his plan of action. On December 14, the agent composed a letter to Bull Head, written in the Lakota language, ordering him to take Sitting Bull. "You must not let him escape under any circumstances," the agent hurriedly wrote in the postscript.

McLaughlin had already shifted his most loyal Indian police, numbering twenty-six men, to a camp located northwest of Sitting Bull's house along Oak Creek. He quickly sent others to join them boosting the total to about forty. Among the group was Lieutenant Bull Head, First Sergeant Shaved Head, Red Tomahawk, Lone Man, and Little Eagle. All were related, one to another, and a few had family ties with Sitting Bull. Lone-man had fought at the Little Big Horn, lived with Sitting Bull at Wood Mountain for two years, and had moved into Sitting Bull's village in the early 1880s. Many of the others had similar backgrounds.

At 4:00 a.m., December 15, Bull Head had his men bow their heads while he led them in a Christian prayer. A few minutes later, they departed for Sitting Bull's house, first striking Grand River above the settlement where they added Gray Eagle to the party, Sitting Bull's brother-in-law. He had had a stormy relationship with the Hunkpapa *blotaunka* ever since their disagreement in Canada. Gray Eagle came now to protect his sisters who were in Sitting Bull's house. As the police hugged the banks of the Grand River, heading eastward, gloom came over many of the riders, for many of them feared the power of the ghost shirts and most expected trouble.

Arriving just before dawn, the heavily armed police party entered Sitting Bull's encampment from the south as dogs barked and a few people glanced out their tepees and makeshift huts. Bull Head headed directly to Sitting Bull's door and knocked. "How, timahel hiyu wo," the chief answered—"all right, come in." Several police quickly entered, and Shaved Head told Sitting Bull that they had come to take him to Standing Rock. Sitting Bull's older wife gave out a shriek, which drew attention, but the chief agreed to go. Attempting to dress in the darkness proved difficult, but finally the party began to exit, Bull Head and Shaved Head on either side of the Hunkpapa *blotaunka.*

Growing nervous, the policemen urged Sitting Bull forward into the dawn and the waiting horses and, unfortunately, a growing crowd of people who watched from the sidelines. Out of this increasingly hostile group, a voice broke the silence. It was Catch-The-Bear, archrival of Bull Head and a leading defender of Sitting Bull: "Just as we had expected all the time. You think you are going to take him. You shall not!" Others joined in intimidating the police, including Sitting Bull's teenage son Crow Foot, who stood in the doorway. Crow Foot, after watching his father being dragged off, suddenly spoke: "You always called yourself a brave chief. Now you are allowing yourself to be taken by the Indian Police."

Sitting Bull stopped walking and seemed to say that he would not go. Bull Head and Shaved Head tightened their grip on the chief's forearms while some of the policemen urged him on through the crowd. Suddenly, Catch-The-Bear wheeled a Winchester rifle from under his blanket and fired into Bull Head's side. Almost simultaneously, Bull Head fired his forty-five revolver into the back of Sitting Bull. As the Hunkpapa *blotaunka* fell, Red Tomahawk put the barrel of his pistol to the back of the chief's head and fired. Sitting Bull fell stone dead on his face in front of his cabin.

Other shots rang out in quick succession as a fierce gun battle erupted. Among the police, Little Eagle, Hawk Man, and Broken Arm fell, killed almost at point-blank range. But the dying policemen took many of Sitting Bull's ghost dancers with them. Lone Man clubbed Catch-The-Bear and then shot him while he lay on the ground. As they fell, mortally wounded policemen fired haphazardly into the crowd, killing Bob Tail Bull's son, Spotted Horn, Brave Thunder, Joe Shield, and finally, Jumping Bull.

Bull Head and Shaved Head both survived, but they lay bleeding profusely among the dead and dying. Dragged into Sitting Bull's house, and aware that they were dying, they soon stumbled onto Crow Foot, hiding near the bed. As Loneman and other police inside pulled him out, he pleaded for his life: "Uncle, I want to live." Loneman asked Bull Head what to do. The lieutenant, now in agony, said: "Kill him, they killed me." Loneman hit him along the head with his rifle and sent him sprawling. As the boy stumbled in the doorway, several shots rang out and he fell outside, dead.

As the darkness turned to a gray dawn, Sitting Bull's followers fled into the trees on the north and south of the village. There they fired on the police, occasionally trying to launch an all-out attack. One dancer, wearing a ghost shirt, refused to retreat. He was Crow Woman. Riding a black horse, he repeatedly charged the now entrenched agency police, being driven back by a hail of bullets. Not a cartridge touched either him or his horse.

Though somewhat outnumbered, the police were aware that Colonel Drum had taken the precaution to send two companies of troops to their support. The cavalry, under command of Captain Edmond Fetchet, finally arrived as light appeared, sending the ghost dancers scurrying west. On the ground outside Sitting Bull's cabin lay eight dead Indians, and inside were four others. Bull Head and Shaved Head would remain alive long enough to reach the post hospital, but their deaths would bring the number of killed to fourteen. Fetchet failed to pursue the dancers any farther since Sitting Bull, the object of his mission, lay sprawled out before him.

The weather had finally turned cold, and Fetchet ordered the bodies of the Indian police and Sitting Bull loaded into a wagon for transport back to Standing Rock. Several Indian policemen protested the carrying of their comrades in the same conveyance with Sitting Bull. As a young lieutenant mediated the dispute, a grieving relative of one of the dead policemen straddled Sitting Bull's corpse and smashed in his face with a large piece of scrap wood. The debaters soon reached a compromise. It was decided to dump the mutilated body of Sitting Bull on the bottom of the wagon and pile the policemen on top of him.

The suppression of the ghost dance at Standing Rock had foreordained the end of Sitting Bull's world, for the Lakota leader did not wish to live in the world that the white man was building. This worshipper of sacred stones, master of visions, and practitioner of the sun dance had tasted the world of the *wasicun*, and prayed to return to his own. Even in death, he left a spiritual legacy for his people, put to song by a fellow member of the Fox Society.

> Friends, take fresh courage,
> This is my country, I loved it,
> Sitting Bull, saying this, has passed away
>
> Friends, take fresh courage,
> As for me, I'm helpless,
> Sitting Bull saying this, has passed away

CHAPTER 6

Epilogue

❖
❖

The death of Sitting Bull brought considerable unrest to Standing Rock and the surrounding Indian communities. Fortunately for Agent McLaughlin and Colonel Drum, the weather turned colder and snow appeared in the week before Christmas, making it nearly impossible for the ghost dancers associated with Sitting Bull to carry on their movement. Some had no intentions of doing so anyway, for dead relatives had never returned as promised, and bullets had killed seven dancers. Near the agency, the Indians turned to burying the dead.

The day following the carnage on Grand River, a wagon train bearing the bodies of the dead police and Sitting Bull approached Fort Yates. While the columns of soldiers marched into the fort, the contingent of police escorted their fallen comrades into Standing Rock, where various Catholic and Protestant clergy made arrangements for burial. On the afternoon of December 17, the clergy held joint services for the dead at the small, newly built Congregational Church. Burial plots had been procured in the Catholic mission cemetery, the bodies being lowered into their final resting places as a company of army infantry fired volleys into the air. A few female relatives mourned in the traditional way, wailing and cutting their hair.

Sitting Bull's corpse received no such honors, however, since the Catholic priest at Standing Rock had refused to allow him to be interred in the church cemetery. The families of the various police officers killed in the line of duty also protested. Two of those families, those of Shaved Head and Bull Head, had waited in agony as these men died in the hospital on the very day in which the others were buried.

Sitting Bull's body had been moved to a small shack behind the agency hospital where late on the afternoon of December 17, John Franklin Waggoner, assisted by prison labor from Fort Yates, fashioned a small wooden box—two feet square by six feet four inches—and placed Sitting Bull in it. Several members of the burial party sought souvenirs, one pulling off the chief's breach cloth and another seizing his leggings. Nearly naked, Waggoner counted seven bullet holes in the corpse, testimony contradicted by the official report of the post surgeon, Horace H. Deeble, who reported only three. The prisoners poured a mixture of chloride of lime and muriatic acid over the remains, nailed the lid shut, and carried the box out to the far northeast corner of the post cemetery. Here, in an unmarked hole, they deposited Sitting Bull in a prayerless ceremony that took only a few minutes. The lime was deemed necessary to keep the grave robbers of a civilized society away from the remains that would have been valuable souvenirs.

To prevent any further bloodshed, Colonel Drum quickly ordered the military units at his disposal into the field, both cavalry and infantry. They scouted up the Cannonball and Grand Rivers in the week before Christmas, meeting absolutely no resistance. Captain Javan B. Irvine, who commanded an infantry company stationed at Fort Abraham Lincoln, found nothing but despair and hunger among the Indians he encountered. At first, his reports in the form of letters to his wife, poured out with sympathy for the families of the Indian police. Irvine had spoken with many of the survivors of the fight on Grand River, and he blamed Sitting Bull for the carnage.

As Christmas passed, however, Captain Irvine's letters changed. The whole campaign seemed more ludicrous to him with each passing day. He began to question whether the Lakotas at Sitting Bull's camp ever intended to cause trouble. The dance had broken up most of the schools and churches built by the missionaries, but they could easily be started again. The most serious damage caused by the ghost dance, in Irvine's opinion, was actually to the agricultural efforts of the Indians. The captain saw despair everywhere. Hungry Indians often came into Irvine's camp in late afternoon to beg meals from the cooks. Many feared going into Standing Rock. McLaughlin had little to give them anyway.

In uncharacteristic fashion, Captain Irvine increasingly blamed the Indian agents and the military for the disaster. "Is not this war upon the frightened heathen a ridiculous outrage?" he wrote to his wife on December 29. "If we are kept out here all winter on the warpath, it will be because the higher authorities are ashamed to acknowledge that the great movement [of troops] is a mistake." That movement had grown to include over three thousand men, stationed mostly at the various Indian agencies.

Certainly one of the results of the troop movement had been the exodus of several hundred Hunkpapa Indians from the reservation. Some of them had joined relatives then encamped on a tributary of the Cheyenne River called Cherry Creek. Here, many joined the Minneconjou leader Big Foot, who had been dancing the ghost dance since the fall. Yet these Hunkpapas were hungry and already tired of running from the military. When Captain J. H. Hurst came among them offering terms of surrender, 227 returned with him, reaching Fort Bennett on the Missouri River on December 24.

But a considerable number of Hunkpapas—certainly over one hundred people—remained with Big Foot and his people. They had camped farther up the Cheyenne River and, though intending to surrender, the group had been frightened into fleeing south by the movement of a large number of army troops near Fort Bennett. As Big Foot and his group of Min-neconjous and Hunkpapas fled south, they sent runners to find the camp of Kicking Bear and Short Bull. Unfortunately, the scouts arrived too late since the ghost dancers in the stronghold had determined to surrender at Pine Ridge and had already departed for home. Alone, and aware that a large army was now in the field against them, Big Foot surrendered his party to Major Samuel Whiteside and his troops of the Seventh Cavalry on December 28. Though these cavalry troops were part of Custer's old regiment, hardly a man under Whiteside's command had known the celebrated colonel.

Now close to Pine Ridge Agency, Whiteside moved his captured Indians to a small Creek called Wounded Knee, where other reinforcements joined him. Overall command fell to Colonel James Forsyth, who had eight cavalry troops, scouts, and four Hotchkiss guns (light artillery)—in all 470 men—to control a mere 106 warriors, 38 of them being close relatives of Sitting Bull. Although a few of these Indians still remained advocates of the ghost dance, the camp contained roughly four hundred women and children. Many wanted nothing more than to go home.[1]

The next day, the same in which Captain Irvine would write of the injustice of the war, the troops of the Seventh Cavalry surrounded and attempted to disarm the followers of Big Foot. Colonel Forsyth and his staff were in no mood for arguing. The night before, they had ordered the Indians to camp on the plain just above the creek, where they could easily be watched. A small, dry ravine ran behind the camp into the creek, the only cover in the immediate vicinity. But Forsyth

---

[1] Agent McLaughlin reported to the commissioner of Indian Affairs on January 9, 1891 that 372 Indians were still absent from his reservation. Two hundred and twenty-seven were prisoners at Cheyenne River Agency, and most of the rest were likely in Big Foot's camp.

placed his troops on all sides of the Indians, completely sur-rounding them. Even though the majority of the Lakota men possessed arms, Forsyth had already collected over forty weapons when a lone *wicasa wakan* resisted. His shot in the air ignited the troops who opened fire.

While the few Hunkpapa and Minneconjou men in camp tried to defend themselves, the troopers rained down a mur-derous fire, killing indiscriminately. The four Hotchkiss guns raked the camp, each firing nearly fifty rounds of explosive shells per minute. In an hour, two hundred Sioux, including Big Foot and many of Sitting Bull's people, lay mangled on the frozen ground. While many women and children scurried into the ravine to escape the killing, troopers of the Seventh Cav-alry followed them, shooting women and children on the open prairie several miles from the camp. Colonel William Shafter, who commanded the First Infantry, later reported the finding of the bodies of two Indian women and two children some eight miles from the scene, empty cartridges laying nearby "bearing the stamp of the United States Arsenal."

A howling blizzard soon descended on Wounded Knee, making rescue difficult. Troopers did try to cart off the many wounded to the hospital at Pine Ridge, only two dozen miles away, but they gave priority to their own men. Five days after the massacre, two Lakota babies were discovered still clutched by their dead mothers. Both, along with seventy wounded In-dians, later died at the hospital. The Seventh Cavalry suffered eighty killed and wounded, most being hit by friendly fire and the Hotchkiss guns. As Colonel Shafter later claimed, Wounded Knee was "The most damnable outrage ever com-mitted by United States troops."

The Wounded Knee Massacre did have a chilling effect on all the Dakota reservations. Mary Collins, who returned to Grand River in the spring of 1891, found the residue of people there anxious to become Christians. Many would join the Catholic Church in the months that followed. Nevertheless, Collins found her little school house suddenly inundated with Lakota churchgoers, two hundred crowding in each Sunday to hear her sermons. Other churches had to be organized, one forming at Little Oak Creek. One Bull joined this congregation in 1891. He did so after writing a long letter to McLaughlin in which he denounced Sitting Bull and asked the agent how he could "raise himself in the estimation of everybody." By 1899, One Bull had become a deacon in the church. Wakutemani, one of Collins's first male converts from the Sitting Bull community, was his minister.

Through this transition to the new life, the image of Sitting Bull followed a curvaceous route. A eulogy, published just days after his death in the *New York World*, proclaimed him to be "counsellor of chiefs, the Warwick behind the throne . . . the oracle of mysteries and of knowledge hidden from the mass." Special attention was given to his relationship with *Wakantanka*, the Great Spirit. "That the gods of his race found in him a high priest faithful to his trust none may ever deny. He lived and he has died, a red man true to his office and his race."

Nevertheless, Agent McLaughlin and others did their best to denigrate the name and deeds of Sitting Bull. In interview after interview, McLaughlin pressed the general belief that Sitting Bull never possessed much support among the Hunkpapa people and that he was actually quite unintelligent. Gall, Crow King, and John Grass emerged as McLaughlin's heroes. Indeed, McLaughlin ultimately claimed that Sitting Bull had fled from the Battle of the Little Big Horn, a coward. Partly to vindicate his own role in the ghost dance affair, McLaughlin finally recorded his views of Sitting Bull in his memoirs, published in 1910 as *My Friend the Indian*. For years, it became the standard source for the history of the events surrounding Wounded Knee and Sitting Bull's role in it.

McLaughlin became so enamored with the truth of this fiction that while he remained in office he made every effort to blot out the very existence of Sitting Bull. He repeatedly refused requests to mark the grave site where the chief was buried (a permanent marker would be placed near the site in the 1920s), and in fact, the site became more and more difficult to find. Even so, every spring, flowers mysteriously appeared on or near the grave, to the agent's great consternation.

After McLaughlin's retirement, several of Sitting Bull's relatives from Grand River, headed by Gray Eagle's son, lobbied to have the chief's remains moved to South Dakota. With help from members of the Mobridge, South Dakota business community, a party descended on the grave site one night in the spring of 1953, and disinterred what they believed to be Sitting Bull's bones. They reburied the remains near Mobridge, along the edge of the great reservoir that covered what was once the mouth of Grand River. Undoubtedly to prevent further raids from North Dakota commercialists, they filled the hole with several tons of steel and concrete.

The controversy ignited by the midnight grave robbers led to several archaeological investigations near the old grave site at Fort Yates. After a careful search, scholars from North Dakota concluded that whatever bones had been illegally expropriated, they did not constitute the remains of Sitting Bull. Just where the last *blotaunka* of the Hunkpapa Sioux lays, then, may never be known. Much like Columbus, Sitting Bull in death became a man tugged by history in this direction and that, and suffering the fate of having at least two different tombs.

Yet it certainly would have pleased Sitting Bull to know that his people never forgot him. At the height of the great drought that swept the plains in the 1930s, the federal government launched a "New Deal" for the American Indian, ending the prohibition against dancing. When the drought's stranglehold seemed to be at its worst, One Bull wrote a long letter to Walter Stanley Campbell, a writer and professor of literature at the University of Oklahoma. One Bull asked of Campbell that he return Sitting Bull's *wotawe*, or charm, that had been loaned to him. Campbell complied.

After the precious charm reached One Bull at Standing Rock in the summer of 1936, he organized and conducted the first sun dance performed at the agency in fifty-four years. One Bull later told a friend that he did not think that dancing the sun dance in any way conflicted with his understanding of Christianity. As One Bull whirled around the dance pole with Sitting Bull's *wotawe* in hand, he prayed for rain. And it rained.

A Note on Source Material

It goes without saying that this biography owes much to those writers and scholars who came before. A list of the many books and articles about the Lakota Sioux people and Sitting Bull's life as a leader would fill many pages. Suffice it to say that a recent biography by Robert M. Utley, entitled *The Lance and Shield: The Life and Times of Sitting Bull* 1993, is by far the best single volume that outlines in detail the American advance onto the northern plains, the development of policy towards the Sioux people, the plains wars, the inauguration of the reservation system and finally, the Ghost Dance and the tragedy at Wounded Knee. Utley's interpretation of Sitting Bull, the person, follows the views of Stanley Vestal's earlier *Sitting Bull: Champion of the Sioux*, 1932, albeit using more documentation.

The Walter S. Campbell Collection at the University of Oklahoma's Western History Library is the most important primary source for Sitting Bull's life. Campbell, an English professor who published under the name Stanley Vestal, wrote the first scholarly biography of Sitting Bull, using as source material four years of field research which he conducted in both North and South Dakota starting in 1928. In particular, he interviewed White Bull and One Bull, Sitting Bull's nephews. This research, along with the interviews of many other Sitting Bull contemporaries, are in Boxes 104 and 105 of the Campbell collection. Boxes 106 through 115 contain a plethora of documents, including the reports of military and Indian Bureau officers.

Campbell's collection of documents, although thorough, can be augmented by several major collections. Correspondence from the various Indian agents is found on microfilm in Record Group 75, Bureau of

Indian Affairs Records. The following are useful: Grand River Agency, 1871–1975, Red Cloud Agency, 1871–1880, Dakota Superintendency, 1861–1880 and Upper Platte Agency, 1846–1870. Various collections from the Adjutant General's Letters Papers, Received files, Record Group 94, are also available on microfilm, including reports from the various Indian agencies and information on the many battles fought between government troops and the Sioux. The main files to consult are in Microcopy 619 and Microcopy 666.

Other manuscript collections provide information on Sitting Bull's captivity, his years at Grand River and his participation in the Ghost Dance. Most useful are the Thomas L. Riggs Papers (including many letters from missionary Mary Collins) and the Javon B. Irvine Papers in the United Church of Christ Archives, Western History Collections, Augustana College. The Mary Collins Papers and the Doane Robinson Papers at the South Dakota Historical Society also contain some information on the reservation period. Finally, the James McLaughlin Papers at Assumption Abby Archives, Richardton, North Dakota, offer the views of the Standing Rock Indian Agent. These papers are on microfilm and are available at the University of Oklahoma Library.

One last source for information are the various newspapers published in both Minnesota and the Dakotas. I wish to thank Alan R. Woolworth, Research Fellow, Minnesota Historical Society, for allowing me to access his immensely useful newspaper collection, files that contain articles on Sitting Bull and the Sioux situation from both prominent and obscure newspapers as well as little known journals from the day.

Index